DISCARD

Legend

● Indian / Inuit Community

— Provincial Boundaries

--- Canadian / U.S. Border

0   200   400
km

LEGACY

Indian Treaty Relationships

by
Richard T. Price

Plains Publishing Inc.

Cataloguing in Publication Data

Price, Richard, 1942-

   ISBN 0-920985-31-9
   Legacy Indian Treaty Relationships

Includes bibliographical references.
ISBN 0-92085-31-9

   1. Indians of North America--Canada--Treaties
2. Indians of North America--Canada--Legal
status, laws, etc.   3. Indians of North America--
Canada--Government relations--1951-
I. Title

KE7702.7.P74 1990   342.71'0872   C90-090277-9

Plains Publishing Inc.
15879 - 116 Ave.,
Edmonton, Alberta
Canada T5M 3W1

Cover design: Christopher Shaw
Cover photography: Rolf Albert
Maps and graphs: Gundra Kucy, Christopher Shaw
Editor: Valerie Harlton

Printed and bound in Canada

Acknowledgements _____

The manuscript for this book was developed under the auspices of Alberta Education through monies provided by the Native Education Project.

The author and publisher would like to acknowledge and express appreciation to the following individuals and organizations:

Alberta Foundation for the Literary Arts;

Alison Beal, The Fur Institute of Canada;

Dennis Dreaver, National Capitol Commission;

Enoch Cree Nation;

Ethnology Program, Provincial Museum of Alberta, Alberta Culture and Multiculturalism, for permission to photograph artifacts H88.94.71A and H62.2.329 B;

Ron Gauthier, Native Network News;

Christiane Gour, Education Branch, Indian and Northern Affairs Canada;

Wayne Hanna and Fred Jobin, Indian and Northern Affairs Canada;

Lee Mingo, Syncrude Canada;

Kelly Nolin, British Columbia Archives and Record Service;

Lisa Patterson, Doug Payette and Sarah Montgomery, National Archives of Canada;

France Poirer, Hydro Quebec;

Saddle Lake Nation and St. Paul Education: Peter Buggins, Gloria McGilvery, Joan Makokis, Dave Dwonanco, Gloria Zukwisky and Ted Cabaj;

Siska Nation and the County of Wheatland #16: Mervin Wolf Leg, Audrey Breaker, Frieda White and Camelia Hume;

Treaty 8 Commission and High Prairie School Division #48: Nora Yellowknee, Lee Davies, Mary Collins, Leonard Young, Robert Cree and Richard Davis;

Dana Wagg, Windspeaker;

Lynnette Walton, Glenbow Institute;

Mike Zeppieri, Canapress Photo Service;

Research and Writing Advisors:

Helen Wood, Researcher and Editor;

Dr. John E. Foster, Professor of History, University of Alberta;

Jennie Lee Price, high school student, Strathcona Composite High School;

Maxine Newbold, high school teacher, Harry Ainlay Composite High School;

Joann S. Morris, Advisor, Alexander's Kipohtakaw Education Centre;

Liz Warman, Consultant, Edmonton Public School Board;

Dr. Donald Massey, Professor, Elementary Education, University of Alberta;

Indian Association of Alberta Consultants:

Regina Crowchild, President;

Harold Cardinal, Native Studies Instructor;

Richard Davis, Treaty Eight Vice-president;

Percy Potts, Treaty Six Vice-president;

Andrew Bear Robe, Treaty Seven;

Representatives:

Walter Janvier, Executive Director;

Frances Weaselfat, Education Portfolio;

Indian Elders from Treaty areas Six, Seven and Eight;

Alberta's Department of Education:

Project Managers:

Merv Kowalchuk, Director, Native Education Project;

Philip Boyle, Consultant, Native Education Project;

Dennis Wall, Consultant, Native Education Project;

Project Consultants:

Ron Cammaert, Associate Director, Curriculum Branch;

Douglas D. Burns, Coordinator, Secondary Social Studies, Curriculum Branch;

Jim Miller, Consultant, Curriculum Branch;

Bob McClelland, Consultant, Curriculum Branch; and

Alexandra Hildebrandt, Consultant, Curriculum Support Branch.

Dedication ━━━━━━━━━━━━━━━━━━━━━━

This book is dedicated to my family and to a small group of Indian Elders.

My family members, my wife, Helen, and my children, Jennie Lee and Christopher, have been a constant source of encouragement and support.

Three Indian elders — Raven Makkannaw (Treaty Six), Rufus Goodstriker (Treaty Seven), and Dan McLean (Treaty Eight) — have given me knowledge and inspiration.

I feel deeply grateful to these people for making the writing and completion of this book possible.

Photo Credits

Codes:
AMMSA: Aboriginal Multi-Media Society of Alberta
APAB: Alberta Public Affairs Bureau, AV and Exhibit Services
BC Archives: British Columbia Archives and Record Service
Canapress: Canapress Photo Service
Glenbow: Glenbow Institute, Calgary
Granger: The Granger Collection, New York
INAC: Indian and Northern Affairs Canada
NAC: National Archives of Canada
PAA: Provincial Archives of Alberta
PAB: Public Affairs Bureau

Front Cover: (Treaty Seven) NAC, RG 10, Volume 1848, IT 310, IA 163
p. 3: Courtesy of P. E. Frere, NAC (C56481)
p. 4: Courtesy of Granger (4E811.20)
p. 5: Courtesy of Take Stock Inc., Calgary
p. 10: Courtesy of Glenbow (NA-1323-4)
p. 11: Courtesy of Glenbow (NA-1185-5)
p. 12: Courtesy of Glenbow (NA-3242-1)
p. 13: Courtesy of Glenbow (NA1241-10)
p. 15: "Western Canada: The New Eldorado," Poster, Courtesy of NAC, Record of the Department of the Interior, Immigration Branch, RG 76, Vos 243, File No. 161973, N.D.
p. 16: Courtesy of Glenbow (NA-698-3)
p. 21: Courtesy of Henry Standing Alone
p. 22: Courtesy of Manitoba Archives, Barber Collection (150)
p. 23: Courtesy of PAA, E. Brown Collection
p. 24: Courtesy of PAA, E. Brown Collection (B.1733)
p. 27: Courtesy of PAA (A.11,332)
p. 28: Courtesy of Royal Ontario Museum, Paul Kane
p. 31: Courtesy of Glenbow (NA-3421-9)
p. 32: Courtesy of PAA
p. 34: Courtesy of PAA, E. Brown Collection (B.2864)
p. 35: Courtesy of PAA, E. Brown Collection (B.5224)
p. 36: Courtesy of PAA, E. Brown Collection (B.2093)
p. 38: Courtesy of Glenbow (NA-2839-5)
p. 39: Courtesy of Glenbow (NA-949-34)
p. 40: Courtesy of PAA (A.7072)
p. 42: Courtesy of Glenbow (NA-1358-1)
p. 47: Courtesy of PAB
p. 48: Courtesy of Granger (4E645.03)
p. 49: Courtesy of Glenbow (NA-249-42)
p. 51: Courtesy of NAC (C8133)
p. 59: Courtesy of PAA (B.10102)
p. 60: Courtesy of PAA, E. Brown Collection
p. 61: Courtesy of PAA, E. Brown Collection (B.844)
p. 64: Courtesy of Glenbow (M1837)
p. 65: Courtesy of Glenbow (NA-491-2)
p. 66: Courtesy of BC Archives (HP82610)
p. 67: Courtesy of PAA (A.4287)
p. 70: Courtesy of Provincial Museum of Alberta
p. 73: Courtesy of NAC (C121918)
p. 77: Courtesy of Canapress
p. 78: Courtesy of Canapress
p. 79: Courtesy of INAC
p. 82: Courtesy of the Supreme Court of Canada
p. 83: Courtesy of Canapress
p. 84: Courtesy of Canapress
p. 85: Courtesy of Canapress
p. 88: Courtesy of Hydro Quebec (L63)
p. 89: Courtesy of Paul Taillefer, NAC (PA 129351)
p. 93: Courtesy of Windspeaker
p. 95: Courtesy of APAB
p. 96: Courtesy of Syncrude Canada
p. 99: Courtesy of Canapress
p. 100: Courtesy of AMMSA
p. 101: Courtesy of Canapress
p. 104: Courtesy of Canapress
p. 107: Courtesy of PAA (J.3615/1)
p. 109: Courtesy of Windspeaker
p. 110: Courtesy of Windspeaker
p. 111: Courtesy of Canapress
p. 113: Courtesy of Windspeaker
p. 120: Courtesy of Windspeaker
p. 123: Courtesy of Dave Olecko Photos, Calgary Herald
p. 125: Courtesy of INAC
p. 126: Courtesy of Canapress
p. 130: Courtesy of Canapress
p. 135: Courtesy of Henry Standing Alone

Foreword

The Indian Association of Alberta is very aware of the need to educate the people of Canada and the world of the history of Indian people. This book, *Legacy Indian Treaty Relationships* by Richard T. Price, provides an opportunity for younger students in Canadian High Schools to gain some insight, and also, hopefully, to better understand the Indian perspective of the treaties with the Crown.

The Indian Association of Alberta stresses the need for a clearer understanding of the First Nation/Crown relationship . . . one that respects our view. This scholarly text will assist those of you who are interested in this area of study. We must, however, caution that there is still much work that needs to be done on clarifying the treaty legacy. The treaty legacy, as yet, is unresolved. The treaties remain living documents to the Indian people.

We are aware that there will be other books and scholarly texts written on this subject in the future. Nevertheless, we are pleased that this text is being published to provide the user an insight into the historical agreements between the Aboriginal First Nations and the British Crown.

History has taught the Indian people that with the continuing debate about the future of Canada, we are all too often ignored. My sincere hope is that this will not continue unabated.

On behalf of the Indian Association of Alberta and its Board of Directors, Executive and Senate, I would like to thank everyone who assisted in the completion of this text. In particular, I thank Richard Price, the writer, for his contribution to our endeavour to have afforded to us our rightful recognition as the First Nations of this land.

Regena Crowchild
President

Contents ━━━━━━━━━━━━━━━━━━━━━━━━

Preface   i
Introduction   ii
About this Book   iii

Section I   Historical Background   **1**

Chapter 1 Treaty Relationships   **3**

    Unit 1   Why do we have Indian treaties in Canada?   4
    Unit 2   What was the relationship before the treaties?   10
    Unit 3   How did eastern Canada view the prairies and its Indian peoples?   15
    Unit 4   How did the government and the Indian tribes view the treaties?   19

Chapter 2 Northern Treaties — Treaty Eight Case Study   **27**

    Unit 1   How were the northern tribes different from the prairie Indians?   28
    Unit 2   Why did the government finally negotiate Treaty Eight?   34
    Unit 3   Did each side get what they wanted from the treaties?   38

Chapter 3 Historical Overview   **47**

    Unit 1   How did each side understand the treaties?   48
    Unit 2   Did the Indian treaties turn out the way the negotiators expected?   59
    Unit 3   What did the government impose on the Indians?   64
    Unit 4   How did provincial governments get involved in treaty promises?   69
    Unit 5   How did the Indians react to government neglect of treaties?   72

Section II   Contemporary Situation   **75**

Chapter 4 Policy Changes and Land Claims   **77**

    Unit 1   What key events of the 1970s made changes in Indian policy
           possible?   78

Unit 2   Did the James Bay and Northern Quebec Agreement of 1975
        indicate a change in policy?   87

Unit 3   Why are there still outstanding land claims in areas
        which have treaties?   93

Chapter 5   Current Controversies   **99**

Unit 1   How did the Constitution Act of 1982 affect aboriginal
        and treaty rights?   100

Unit 2   Is Indian self-government a treaty right?   107

Unit 3   Why is Indian control of Indian education important?   116

Unit 4   Is post-secondary education a treaty right?   119

Chapter 6   Treaty Relationship Renewal   **123**

Unit 1   How will treaty and aboriginal rights issues be resolved
        in Canada?   122

Unit 2   What negotiating approaches have been effective, and what values
        and relationships must be considered?   128

Unit 3   .Why does Canada need a Royal Commission on Native Issues?   130

Epilogue   **133**

Appendix   **137**

Notes   **144**

Glossary   **146**

Select Bibliography   **149**

Index   **152**

Preface

Indian treaty rights and claims are a source of confusion for many Canadians. Yet these same treaty rights and relationships are what Canadian Treaty Indians base their hopes on for their present and future well-being. Clearly, Indian treaties and the issues linked with the treaties need to be understood by all Canadians.

Several outstanding Canadians, including former Governor General Edward Schreyer, have described these issues as "unfinished business" for Canada. A series of First Ministers Conferences on Aboriginal and Treaty Rights was held from 1982 to 1987. When completed, many outstanding issues remained unresolved. With this disagreement at the highest level, it is necessary for all Canadians to understand the differences separating the federal and provincial governments, and Canada's first peoples. Closer to home, land claims, treaty right to land, education, and self-government have proven to be difficult issues to resolve. If mutually-acceptable agreements and understandings could be developed, a potential would exist for new relationships. This would be a new legacy for future generations in Canada.

Placed in this broader context, a resolution of Indian treaty rights issues can be viewed as a responsibility of citizenship for all Canadians. Moreover, if Canada, as an independent nation, expects to have a meaningful role in international affairs, other nations will rightly inquire if Canada has its own "house in order" with the aboriginal Canadians. Young Canadians will have, and in many ways already have, an important role to play in shaping Canada for the future.

Awareness of treaty negotiations, historical development and the present situation will enable everyone to better understand the hopes and concerns of Indian peoples today.

Introduction ────────────────

Increasing numbers of demonstrations and confrontations initiated by Indian communities in Canada in the late 1980s and the summer of 1990 signal a change in Canadian society and politics. When the issues involve treaty and aboriginal rights, Canada's original inhabitants are no longer willing to maintain endless patience with governments.

Indian bands across Canada, including the Haidas on the Queen Charlotte Islands, the Lubicons in Alberta, the Bear Island Band in northern Ontario and the Mohawk in Quebec, are blockading roads. The message to the rest of society seems to be that "enough is enough."

A number of questions are raised by these events: Can Indian demands be accommodated in the Canadian confederation? Why do governments sometimes display a responsiveness, and yet often an unwillingness to act? Are the issues related to treaty rights simply a little-known part of Canadian politics and culture? Could Indian leaders and communities be more effective in expressing their positions and concerns? How do citizens in a democracy affect change on deeply-felt issues? If governments do not respond more quickly and negotiate with the elected Indian leaders (who are often more moderate), will the governments have to face more militant Indian band members instead?

As we examine the historical background and contemporary situation underlying these and other questions, it will be helpful to begin thinking about and trying to express our own feelings about these issues in a new and open way. Perhaps the younger generation of Canadians, both Native and non-Native, may be able to suggest alternative ways of overcoming these conflicts within our society.

Rights and the accompanying responsibilities are matters that should receive due consideration by all individuals and peoples who make up Canada in the late 20th century. Moreover, the decisions that are taken on these controversial issues of Native rights in the 1990s will influence the kind of legacy that we pass on to future generations.

About This Book

Legacy Indian Treaty Relationships is consistent with the goal of developing a critically-thinking citizen, who is able to use a variety of problem-solving, research and inquiry methods to generate alternative solutions and make informed choices.

The format of the book involves two distinct, yet inter-related sections, dealing both with the past and the present. Each section is divided into three chapters, which in turn are divided into a number of units.

Each unit begins with a focus question, which is followed by key issues and concrete examples. The goal of each unit is to ensure the students have a clear grasp of what is at stake, especially the perspectives of aboriginal peoples, and the views of federal/provincial governments or other interested parties. Discussion questions on the content of each unit and analysis questions for further research are included at the end of each unit.

It is recognized that there are several different potential ways of resolving issues. Students will be encouraged to think about several alternatives, the possible processes for resolution, and the changes (attitudinal and institutional) necessary to develop longer-term, mutually-acceptable solutions.

The changing nature of the relationships between Indian peoples and the larger Canadian majority is not well-known. These relationships between peoples and the conflicts over treaty rights will be on the political agenda of Canada in the future.

The fact that there are conflicting or differing views on treaty rights illustrates their controversial nature. Controversial matters are often referred to as issues. For you, currently studying in high schools in Canada, these issues will be a part of the media coverage in the days, months and years ahead. These matters are of concern to all Canadian citizens from all backgrounds.

Within the context of a balanced, even-handed approach to the topics, special attention is given to Native perspectives in *Legacy Indian Treaty Relationships*. There are a number of reasons for this:

- Native perspectives have been neglected or misunderstood in other books;
- Native history and tradition could be a source of inspiration for all Canadians; and ·
- openness to different cultures and values is an ingredient of multiculturalism and contributes to better communication and to Canadian unity.

The questions raised involve a wide spectrum of concerns. These include:

- individual and social ethics;
- peaceful and just relations between a significant minority (Native peoples) and the larger society;
- the relevance of native philosophies;
- strategies of broadening public education and support; and
- the political responsibilities and will on all sides to find mutually-acceptable solutions.

Thus, the Indian treaty rights agenda for the 1990s and beyond is full of difficult, yet exciting and important goals and tasks.

Section I
Historical Background

This book takes a close look at the early relationship between the Canadian Indian peoples and the Europeans using two different historical sources: oral accounts and written history.

Indian cultures have had a very strong oral tradition for centuries. This is how they have preserved their histories, legends and traditions. Some of this information has been collected and written down. These written memories of the past are oral accounts.

One example of an oral account is *Earth Elder Stories*, written by Saulteaux storyteller, Alexander Wolfe. Wolfe tells stories he has the right to tell — those which have been passed down through his family, the descendants of Pinayzitt (Partridge Foot). In the introduction to his book, Wolfe explains the significance of the oral tradition to Indian people:

> From centuries past comes a path. On this path the grandfathers walked as did their grandfathers before them. Each in his time carried the history of their people, their identity and a way of life. Many years have passed since I heard the stories from the grandfathers. The stories fascinated me as they were told.
>
> Quite often the grandfathers used a saying in the Saulteaux language, '*Mawesha Anishnawbak Keyutotunmok.*' This means, 'In times past the Indian people listened.'

I now know why the grandfathers felt that listening was important. The oral tradition, in which history is embedded, requires the use of memory. The teachings that instruct a person in their identity, their purpose in life, their responsibility and contribution to the well-being of others are put in the memory for safekeeping..The grandfathers wanted young people to listen, to use their minds to the utmost capacity as a storeroom. In later times, when they too became grandfathers, the stories would be passed on to the next generation, ensuring the survival of their history and way of life. As the years passed, the grandfathers passed on. Suddenly there were none. The grandfathers were gone, but not their stories.[1]

Now a grandfather himself, Wolfe writes:

One does not reach this age merely to think of the past, but to have hope and aspirations for the future, and to do something so history and a way of life may continue for the purpose it was intended.[2]

Indian elders try to provide their communities with interpretations of history, which will help the communities survive in the present and the future.

Written history is based on the study and interpretation of old, written documents. Historians have had to struggle with the problem of resolving the differences between oral and written history.

One Canadian historian, George Stanley, expresses his ideas from the perspective of many historians, who have favoured written history. However, Stanley can also see the problems of written history:

I am not prepared to argue whether written or oral history, law or tradition, is the more reliable. Certainly, men's memories are frequently faulty; but documents may be incomplete or ambiguous, or, at the worst, forgeries or outright lies. Who, then, has the whole truth and nothing but the truth? The Indian with his memory, or the white man with his documents? Perhaps both are struggling in the darkness of the past. Whence cometh the light?[3]

The approach used in this book seeks a balance between written and oral tradition, recognizing and respecting the validity of both. The cover of this book symbolizes these different traditions. The spiritual and oral traditions are represented by the pipe and the sweetgrass. The formal and written traditions are represented by the written document and the official seal.

Chapter 1
Treaty Relationships

We are the children of the plains, it is our home, and the buffalo has been our food always. I hope you look upon Blackfeet, Bloods and Sarcees [Stoneys, Peigan] as your children now, and that you will be indulgent and charitable to them. They all expect me to speak now for them, and I trust the Great Spirit will put into their breasts to be a good people — into the minds of the men, women and children, and their future generations.

— Crowfoot, 1877

Why do we have Indian treaties in Canada?

A treaty is an agreement negotiated between two or more nations.

Indian peoples have a long history of treaty making.

Treaties were used by Indian peoples long before the first fur traders or settlers arrived in what is now Canada. Treaties were negotiated to end wars and settle land disputes. Agreements were also made involving trading opportunities and marriage among families of different tribes.

One of the earliest recorded treaties was the Great Law of Peace of the People of the Longhouse, which was negotiated before 1450. This treaty involved the Seneca, Mohawk, Onondaga, Oneida and Cayuga peoples.

It covered 117 articles that governed relationships and customs. It served as a code of law and a form of government. This treaty was passed on orally from generation to generation. It was not until 1880 that it was put in writing.

Treaties and agreements between Indian peoples were passed on orally from generation to generation.

Great Law of Peace
of the People of the Longhouse

I am Tekanawita.

With the statesmen of the League of Five Nations, I plant the Tree of Great Peace.

I plant it in your territory, Atotarho, and the Onondaga Nation, in the territory of you who are Firekeepers.

I name the tree Tsioneratasekowa, the Great White Pine.

Under the shade of this Tree of Great Peace, we spread the soft, white feathery down of the Globe Thistle as seats for you, Atotarho, and your cousin statesmen.

We place you upon those seats, spread soft with the feathery down of the Globe Thistle, there beneath the shade of the spreading branches of the Tree of Great Peace. There shall you sit and watch the Fire of the League of Five Nations. All the affairs of the League shall be transacted at this place before you, Atotarho and your cousin statesmen, by the statesmen of the League of Five Nations.

Roots have spread out from the Tree of Great Peace, one to the north, one to the east, one to the south, and one to the west. These are the Great White Roots, and their nature is Peace and Strength.

If any man or any nation of the Five Nations shall obey the laws of the Great Peace (Kaianerekowa), and shall make this known to the statesmen of the League, they may trace back the roots to the Tree. If their minds are clean, and if they are obedient and promise to obey the wishes of the Council of the League, they shall be welcomed to take shelter beneath the Great Evergreen Tree.

We place at the top of the Tree of Great Peace an eagle, who is able to see afar. If he sees in the distance any danger threatening, he will at once warn the people of the League.

Treaties between Indian peoples were primarily peace treaties to end wars. They established the land or territory that tribes would share. The treaty between the Dakota and Ojibwa communities in Manitoba in 1866 was one example. The Dakota chief, H'damani, explained that:

> . . . the Dakota had acquired from the Ojibwa the right to live in and use the Turtle Mountains; the Ojibwa were often resident there. H'damani gave the chief warrior of the Ojibwa four horses and five sacred pipes in return for the lands.[1]

European peoples have also negotiated treaties among themselves for centuries. While some of their agreements were peace treaties, many of them involved settlements of territorial disputes such as land transactions.

The Treaty of Paris (1763), between the Kings of Britain, France and Spain, ended the Seven Years' War. It also resulted in a transfer of land from France to Britain.

The territories acquired by the British under the Treaty of Paris were set down in the Royal Proclamation of 1763.

This proclamation followed an Indian uprising against the British, lead by Chief Pontiac of the Ottawa nation.

Although Pontiac and his allies lost their war with Britain, the Indians took the position that they

Treaty of Paris
Feb 10, 1763

His Most Christian Majesty renounces all pretensions which he has heretofore formed or might have formed to Nova Scotia or Acadie in all its parts and guaranties the whole to it, and with all its dependencies, to the King of Great Britain: Moreover, his Most Christian Majesty cedes and guaranties to his said Britannick Majesty, in full right, Canada, with all its dependencies, as well as the Island of Cape Breton and all the other islands and coasts in the gulph and river of St. Lawrence, and, in general, everything that depends on the said countries, lands, islands and coasts, with the sovereignty property, possession and all rights acquired by treaty or otherwise, which the Most Christian King and the Crown of France have had until now over the said countries, lands, islands, places, coasts and their inhabitants . . . .

continued to hold the land which they occupied. The Royal Proclamation established that legal right. It also set down guidelines dealing with Indian treaty negotiations.

The Royal Proclamation guaranteed:

1. Indian hunting grounds would be preserved (until treaties were signed);
2. Indian peoples would be protected against fraud by private individuals;
3. the British Monarch held exclusive right to enter into negotiations with Indian peoples;
4. treaty negotiations between the British Monarch and Indian peoples would be conducted at public assemblies; and
5. Indian treaties would be the result of the British Monarch negotiating and purchasing Indian hunting grounds from the Indian peoples.

The Royal Proclamation of 1763

And whereas it is just and reasonable, and essential to our Interests, and the security of our Colonies, that the several Nations or Tribes of Indians with whom We are connected, and who live under our protection, should not be molested or disturbed in the Possession of such Parts of Our Dominions and Territories as, not having been ceded to or purchased by Us, are reserved to them or any of them, as their Hunting Grounds . . .

. . . And Whereas Great frauds and Abuses have been committed in purchasing Lands of the Indians, to the Great Prejudice of our Interests and to the Great Dissatisfaction of the said Indians . . .

. . . We do, with the Advice of our Privy Council, strictly enjoin and require, that no private Person do presume to make any purchase from the said Indians of any Lands reserved to the said Indians, within those parts of our Colonies where, We have thought proper to allow settlement; but that, if at any Time any of the said Indians should be inclined to dispose of the said Lands, the same shall be Purchased only for Us, in our Name, at some public Meeting or Assembly of the said Indians . . .

These principles formed the basis of the British, and later the Canadian government's, legal requirements for Indian treaties. In effect, the Royal Proclamation places a legal obligation on the government when it enters into treaty negotiations with the Indian peoples.

From an Indian perspective, the document is significant because it recognizes Indian nations as nations, in the wording: ". . . the several Nations or Tribes . . . with whom we are connected."

A recent Supreme Court of Canada decision gives some support to this Indian interpretation:

> . . . we can conclude from the historical documents that both Great Britain and France felt that the Indian nations had sufficient independence and played a large enough role in North America for it to be good policy to maintain relations with them very close to those maintained between sovereign nations.[2]

The Supreme Court of Canada also recognizes Indian treaties as being unique forms of treaties. It has stated:

> . . . what characterizes a treaty is intention to create obligations, the presence of mutually-binding obligations and a certain measure of [seriousness].[3]

There were a number of Indian treaties signed in Canada between 1763 and 1867. These early treaties primarily dealt with Indian peoples in southern Ontario, Quebec and the Maritime provinces, and were negotiated by the British government.

Treaty negotiations between the Government of Canada and the Indian tribes began after Confederation. This book focuses on those treaties after 1867 because they were negotiated and signed by Canada.

Negotiations eventually included all of the present-day prairie provinces, British Columbia and the Northwest Territories. The negotiations involved commissioners, who represented the Queen and the federal government. Indian chiefs represented culturally-diverse Indian bands, tribes and nations.

Provincial governments were not normally involved in these negotiations. Under the British North America Act of 1867, the federal government was given constitutional responsibility for "Indians and lands reserved for Indians."

From 1871 to 1877, Indian Treaties One to Seven were negotiated in the prairie provinces and Ontario. Treaties Eight to Eleven were negotiated in northern areas from 1899 to 1921.

Over a period of years, the government regarded treaties with the Indian peoples as primarily land surrender agreements. Indian peoples, on the other hand, viewed the treaties as the foundation of rights, relationships and responsibilities.

Sharing Ideas

1. Compare the Great Law of Peace of the People of the Longhouse with the Treaty of Paris. Note the difference in language and aims.

2. Describe the significance of the Royal Proclamation of 1763. What were the basic points that served as guiding principles for future negotiations?

Investigating Issues

1. How would you describe the Indian view of the treaties?

2. How would you describe the European view of the treaties?

3. Describe the similarities and differences between the two views.

Key Words

British North America Act A statute enacted on March 29, 1867 by the British Parliament providing for the Confederation of Canada.

Commissioners Members of a group authorized to perform certain official duties or functions

Confederation The union of the colonies of British North America to form Canada.

Fraud An act of deceiving or misrepresenting.

Monarch The ruler or head of state.

Negotiate To consult with another to arrive at the settlement of some matter.

Obligation Something one is required to do.

Sovereign Supreme authority over land or people.

Treaty A contract, settlement or agreement arrived at by negotiations.

What was the relationship before the treaties?

It is important to remember that by the time of treaty negotiations in Canada, the Indian people had already experienced over two centuries of European contact as a result of the fur trade. This contact established a relationship that was beneficial to both the European and Indian cultures.

European goods such as blankets, iron kettles, guns and gun powder found their way into Indian culture. Indian skills and knowledge helped the Europeans survive in the new country. The tribes provided furs for trading, as well as food supplies such as fish and game.

A new cultural group, the Metis, was born of this interaction of Indian and European cultures. The early European explorers and traders were primarily men. Some of the European men decided to make Canada their new home, and to start their families. Many of the men married Indian women. The children from these marriages were the ancestors of Canada's Metis people. The name Metis comes from a French word meaning "mixed."

Many aspects of the fur trade ceremonies were carried over into treaty negotiations by the Indian peoples.

The Europeans and Indians were effective bargainers in the economic exchange of the fur trade. A wide measure of respect and equality developed over time.

Cultural and social aspects of trading were borrowed from each other and incorporated in their relationships. Native rituals were carried over into the negotiations. Elaborate ceremonies developed where gifts of the best furs and copper pots were exchanged.

The Metis were often middlemen between the Indian peoples and the new immigrants to Canada.

Underlying feelings of understanding and friendship were developed between the key trading partners. The relationship between the Indian chief and Chief Factor, the head of the trading post, was crucial. It was continually renewed in the trading ceremonies.

Historian John Foster describes the significance of the relationships developed in these ceremonies in this way:

> It demonstrates the acceptance by Indian and white alike of a [close] relationship. Clashes, often violent, occurred; but they remained incidents. The norm was the relationship spelled out in the fur trade ceremony, the . . . 'we' relationship. Between the middleman and the trader, the relationship tended to emphasize equal status and permitted each to make particular demands on the other.[4]

Indian chiefs had already established a relationship of mutual respect and equality in their fur trade dealings with the Europeans before the treaties. The principal chiefs expected, and insisted on, a similar relationship with the Europeans when negotiating treaties. Both parties in treaty negotiations also had a common need for a harmonious relationship.

This desire for harmony was evident in all the speeches during the first day of negotiations of Treaty Six at Fort Carlton, Saskatchewan, in 1876.

Indian representatives began the proceedings with a sacred pipe ceremony. This ceremony was a symbol of friendship and was a significant part of the negotiations.

Lieutenant Governor Alexander Morris was the commissioner responsible for negotiating Treaties Three to Six.

especially from an Indian viewpoint, that the commissioners and chiefs accepted an ongoing relationship with each other. It also meant that truth must be spoken after using the sacred pipe. From the commissioner's perspective, the ceremony meant accepting the friendship of the Indian peoples.

Morris confirmed the importance of relationships by offering a handshake and by stressing heart-to-heart feelings between people:

> My Indian brothers, Indians of the plains, I have shaken hands with you, I shake hands with all of you in my heart. God has given us a good day, I trust his eye is upon us, and that what we do will be for the benefit of his children.[5]

In Treaty Seven negotiations the following year, Chief Crowfoot, the leading chief of the Blackfoot, again emphasized harmonious relationships. Three years before Treaty Seven, the North West Mounted Police (NWMP) had driven the whisky traders away from Blackfoot territory. At the treaty negotiations, Chief Crowfoot expressed the feeling of being part of a new relationship — the Canadian government and the Blackfoot:

> We are the children of the plains, it is our home, and the buffalo has been our food always. I hope you look upon Blackfeet, Bloods and Sarcees [Stoneys, Peigan] as your children now, and that you will be indulgent and charitable to them. They all expect me to speak now for them, and I trust the Great Spirit will put into their breasts to be a good people — into the minds of the men, women and

The pipe was offered to Lieutenant Governor Alexander Morris. He was the government's treaty commissioner for Treaties Three to Six. In a show of respect for the Indian custom, Morris stroked the pipe several times. It was next passed to the other commissioners, who repeated the ceremony. This solemn ceremony signified,

children, and their future generations. The advice given me and my people has proved to be very good. If the Police had not come to the country, where would we all be now? Bad men and whiskey were killing us so fast that very few, indeed, of us would have been left today. The Police have protected us as the feathers of the bird protect it from the frosts of winter. I wish them all good, and trust that all our hearts will increase in goodness from this time forward.[6]

David Laird, the government's commissioner for Treaties Seven and Eight, emphasized the need to feel as brothers in a family and the importance of shaking hands. His opening statement also recognized Indian spirituality and culture:

The Great Spirit has made all things — the sun, the moon, and the stars, the earth, the forests, and the swift running rivers. It is by the Great Spirit that the Queen rules over this great country and other great countries. The Great Spirit has made the white man and the red man brothers, and we should take each other by the hand.[7]

The emphasis placed on the importance of relationships, however, is not to imply that there were no tough negotiations at the treaties. On the contrary, each side bargained hard to get the best deal from their perspective.

Blackfoot Chief Crowfoot expressed the feeling of being part of a new relationship with the Canadian government at Treaty Seven negotiations.

Sharing Ideas

1. Which level of government was ultimately responsible for the negotiation and administration of Indian lands?

2. Give several examples of mutual respect and benefit shown in the negotiations between Indian leaders and government representatives.

Investigating Issues

1. What were the basic interests of the Indian chiefs during treaty negotiations?

2. What were the basic interests of the government commissioners during treaty negotiations?

3. What areas of agreement and disagreement were there between the two sides?

4. How might the areas of disagreement have been resolved?

Key Words

Chief Factor The head of a fur trading organization in a particular location.

Incorporate To unite into one body.

Metis People of mixed North American Indian and European ancestry.

Rituals Established ceremonies.

How did eastern Canada view the prairies and its Indian peoples?

A movement of people and ideas, described as the expansionist movement, began in Ontario in the late 1840s.

The expansionists saw the west as the prime area in which to expand Ontario's successful farming settlement. There was a shortage of farmland in Ontario and new markets were needed for goods produced in eastern Canada.

The expansionists could be called a settler society. In their minds, the west would become "little Ontario." More importantly, it would become part of the glorious expansion of the British Empire.

Morris and Laird, the key treaty commissioners for Treaties Three to Seven, supported, and were a part of, this expansionist movement.

The expansionists' vision was one of boundless development of small farms across the prairies as far as the eye could see. Their overriding concern was to gain rights to the land. They wanted to get on with agricultural development. They considered this a real, or more profitable, use of the land.

The expansionists did not question their right to transform the prairies into farmland. If this change took place at the expense of Indian culture, it was seen as the price of progress.

Eastern Canadian settlers had an ethnocentric view, because they believed in British cultural superiority. They believed that social reform of the Indians was

Posters encouraged many new settlers to move to Canada's prairies.

necessary and that the advantages of their civilized life should outweigh the loss of Indian culture.

The expansionists did have a sense of fair play in relation to the Indians. They disliked the American government making war on the Indians. Acton Burrows, an expansionist, put it this way:

[In Canada, the Indian] knows that he is under the protection of the Great Mother, that her officers will protect him against harm and faithfully carry out the agreements made under the Treaties by which his title to the soil was surrendered to the Crown . [As] a consequence, an Indian war in Canada is unknown.[8]

From 1840 to 1870, the Ontario expansionists had to overcome certain practical problems to convince eastern Canadians and potential investors of the importance of western development.

One problem was to determine if the western land was fertile and suitable for agriculture. This question was examined in the Palliser and Hind expeditions. The answer was essentially positive.

Transportation difficulties, such as providing a way through the rugged Canadian Shield north of Lake Superior, also had to be overcome. Borrowing from experiences in eastern Canada and especially in the United States, a transcontinental railway looked like an obvious solution to this problem.

With these solutions on the drawing board, the movement found more supporters.

Expansion into western Canada became a political priority for Canada's first prime minister, Sir John A. Macdonald.

The building of a transcontinental railway was the obvious solution to providing a transportation link to the expanding west.

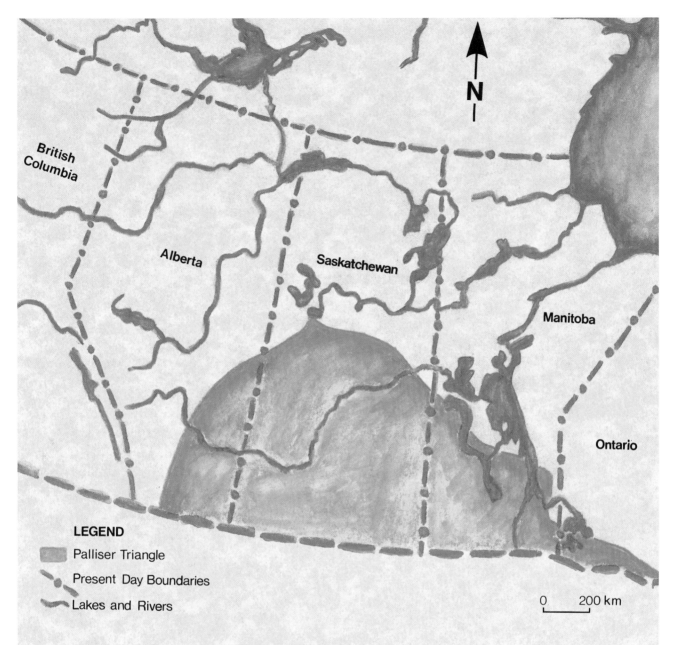

British
Columbia

Alberta

Saskatchewan

Manitoba

Ontario

N

LEGEND

Palliser Triangle

Present Day Boundaries

Lakes and Rivers

0   200 km

Palliser and Hind Expeditions

Between 1857 to 1860, two exploratory expeditions were sent into what is now Manitoba, Saskatchewan and Alberta. Leading these expeditions were Captain John Palliser and Henry Hind.

Their findings were significant to future western development. They discovered two vast sub-districts in the Canadian west.

They reported a rich, fertile belt of land from the Red River district in Manitoba northwest to the Saskatchewan river valley through to the Rocky Mountains. Over time this was viewed as an agrarian Garden of Eden by eastern Canadians. The other area is now known as the Palliser Triangle — a triangular district of very dry plains, which lay to the south of the fertile belt and extended into the United States.

Sharing Ideas

1. What was the Expansionist Movement?

2. Describe the expansionists' view of the Indians.

3. Distinguish between the way Canada and the United States approached concerns of Indian peoples.

Investigating Issues

1. Examine the expansionist movement's impact on Canadian Confederation. What was the impact on western Canada of the transcontinental railway linking Ontario and British Columbia?

2. Study the American treatment of Indian peoples through their Indian treaties. Address the following questions:
   a) How did the size of Indian bands and reserve lands differ between the United States and Canada?
   b) Was the United States more effective or less effective than Canada, in terms of Indian treaty implementation?

Key Words

Ethnocentric The attitude that one's own group or culture is the most important.

Expansionists Members of a political organization in Ontario which advocated expansion into western Canada.

Transform To change in character or condition.

How did the government and the Indian tribes view the treaties?

By the time of Treaty Six and Seven negotiations in 1876 and 1877, the Indians had some very serious concerns.

More and more Canadian settlers were moving onto the prairies. As they moved westward, Indian tribes were being displaced. Although this changed the territories of, and relationships among, the various Indian peoples, they were still prepared to protect their lands until treaties were signed.

The Plains Cree Indians prevented Canadian government surveyors from doing their work by stopping them at the boundary to what the Cree considered their territory.

The buffalo had all but disappeared from the prairies. Other game animals were not as plentiful. Indian tribes from the east and from the United States had already crowded traditional hunting grounds.

Diseases such as smallpox had taken their toll among the Indian people. For the Indians this was a worsening and fearful situation.

Prior to Treaty Six negotiations, messages from the Cree Chiefs Sweetgrass and Kihewin, of the

DECLINE OF THE BUFFALO

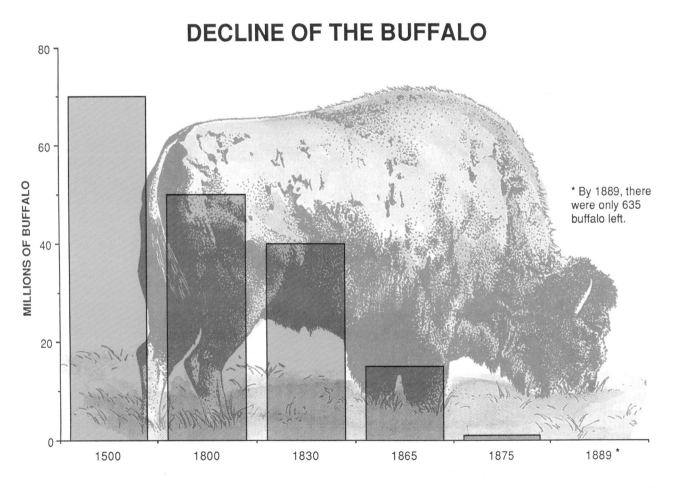

MILLIONS OF BUFFALO

80 — 60 — 40 — 20 — 0

1500   1800   1830   1865   1875   1889 *

* By 1889, there were only 635 buffalo left.

19

Plains Cree, were sent to His Excellency Governor Archibald:

Great Father, I shake hands with you, and bid you welcome. We heard our lands were sold and we did not like it; we don't want to sell our lands; it is our property, and no one has a right to sell them.

Our country is getting ruined of fur-bearing animals, hitherto our sole support, and now we are poor and want help — we want you to pity us. We want cattle, tools, agricultural implements, and assistance in everything when we come to settle — our country is no longer able to support us.

Make provision for us against years of starvation. We have had a great starvation the past winter, and the smallpox took away many of our people, the old, young, and children. We want you to stop the Americans from coming to trade on our lands, and giving firewater, ammunition and arms to our enemies the Blackfeet. Our young men are foolish, it may not last long.

We invite you to come and see us and to speak with us. If you can't come yourself, send someone in your place. We send these words by our Master, Mr. Christie, in whom we have every confidence, — that is all.[9]

Great Father, Let us be friendly. We never shed any white man's blood, and we have always been friendly with the whites, and want workmen, carpenters and farmers to assist us when we settle. I want all my brother, Sweet Grass, asks. That is all.[10]

These were the primary concerns of the most powerful Indian chiefs negotiating the western Indian treaties. They wanted to ensure their physical and cultural survival. A few minor chiefs wanted compensation, or payment, for land and resources. Their demands, however, were not permitted by the main chiefs to jeopardize the entire treaty negotiations. The demand for compensation did force government negotiators to try to put forward the best deal they could offer.

Oral and written accounts of those treaties negotiations question the meaning and nature of the agreements. Today, some question whether a treaty could exist between two parties where there was apparently no "meeting of the minds." Language differences and the resulting need for language translation made treaty negotiations extremely difficult.

Were the English words of the commissioners, translated into Indian languages during

From the Written Version of Treaty Six

The Plain and Wood Cree Tribes of Indians, and all the other Indians inhabiting the district hereinafter described and defined, do hereby cede, release, surrender and yield up to the Government of the Dominion of Canada for Her Majesty the Queen and her successors forever, all their rights, titles and privileges whatsoever, to the lands included within the following limits . . .

The Indian peoples thought of the land spiritually. They saw themselves as the guardians, not the owners, of the land.

treaty negotiations, properly interpreted and understood? Were the messages of the chiefs, spoken in their own languages, fully and properly conveyed? We will never be absolutely certain.

The written terms of the treaties make clear that a legal land transaction, in the form of a land surrender, had occurred in the eyes of the government negotiators.

From the traditional Indian cultural and spiritual perspective, the land *cannot* be bought and sold. The Creator had placed Indians on the land. The Indian peoples saw themselves as the spiritual guardians, not owners, of the land. The land belongs to the Creator or Great Spirit. The right to use the land is a gift to the people. It is their means of survival.

Historian George Stanley acknowledges this traditional

perspective of the Indian people. Stanley uncovered the following statement made by an Indian spokesman at an Indian meeting in 1884 at Fort Carlton, eight years after Treaty Six was signed:

> The Governor Morris comes and tells the Indians we are not coming to buy your land. It is big thing. It is impossible for a man to buy the whole country, we come here to borrow the country, to keep it for you. I want my children to come here and live at peace with you, to live like two brothers. The Indians therefore understand that the country is only borrowed, not bought.[11]

The oral history of the Cree Indians regarding the treaties throws doubt on their understanding of the land transaction. Significantly, the Indian oral tradition views this land transaction as a sharing rather than a sale of land. Plains Cree Indians viewed the reserves as "homelands." The northern Woodland Cree considered the reserves as "the land we kept for ourselves."

One Elder put it this way:

> At the time of the first treaty, my grandfather, Buffalo Chief, was a councillor, along with old Saddleback and Louie Natchowaysis; their chief was Samson. I used to listen to my grandfather. He, too, was issued with a councillor's suit, as they were included with the treaty promises. They were told that, if the land was not suitable for anything, then that portion would not be taken, only the land where the

Treaty Six negotiations at Fort Carlton in 1876, now in present-day Saskatchewan.

The Indian peoples wanted to be free to pursue their traditional way of life after the treaties were signed.

settlers could make their living through agriculture. The commissioners were not to take the game animals, the timber, nor the big lakes — that was for the Indian's means of survival. Also, anything underground would not be given up, only six inches, enough for the settlers to grow crops . . . When the negotiations were complete, the papers were taken away by the commissioners. The mountains were not even mentioned, according to my grandfather, because they would not be useful. These were the terms of reference made by the commissioners at first: 'Anything that cannot be used agriculturally will be yours.' When they took the papers back to Ottawa, they made them so that the government could claim all of Canada.[12]

An overview of interviews with Cree Indian elders in Treaty Six in the early 1970s, compiled by the Indian Association of Alberta, states:

> Treaty Six elders tended to agree that the treaty was an agreement to let white people use the land for farming, and in some cases to let them use timber for building houses and grow grass to feed animals. The treaty commissioners asked only for the use of the depth of soil needed for agriculture; so this is really all the Indians gave up in the treaty. The wild animals and fish were neither asked for, nor given up, as they are the Indians' livelihood. The treaty, then, can be said to concern peoples' livelihoods. [13]

On the other hand, interviews with Treaty Seven elders indicate quite a different understanding of

Poundmaker was a famous Cree leader at the time of Treaty Six.

Queen. They understood that they could hunt anywhere, but were not to interfere with each other.

The elders remembered land being discussed in terms of each tribe being able to choose its own reserve. They later discovered these reserves were much smaller than what they considered to be their own land.

The choice of reserve lands was an important task for Indians and government officials alike. The western prairies and parklands were largely unsurveyed.

The Indians understood that reserve lands would be set aside as homelands. The federal government saw reserves as a temporary place of residence prior to Indian integration into the dominant society.

There was also confusion as to the size of reserve lands. The Canadian government originally only intended to provide small reserves, such as a one-quarter section (64 hectares) for each family of five Indians. Treaties One and Two in Manitoba contained this provision. However, the Ojibwa people in Treaty Three negotiated one square mile (2.59 sq. km) per family of five. The Ojibwa occupied land on the east-west transportation route at Lake of the Woods, near present-day Kenora. This land was needed by the

that treaty. The elders did not remember that the treaty had anything to do with the giving up or sharing of land. In their minds, the terms of the treaty were that, in return for keeping the peace, they would be taken care of by the

Canadian government as a transportation route to western Canada. The Ojibwa used this strategic position to successfully negotiate the increase in the land they received.

As word of this settlement reached the western tribes, the one square mile formula became the standard in future treaty negotiations.

However, it must be remembered that the very idea of dividing up land into square miles was quite unfamiliar to the Indians.

Poundmaker, not yet a chief at the time of Treaty Six negotiations in 1876, reacted to the commissioner's treaty terms of one square mile per family of five, by shouting:

> This is our land! It isn't just a piece of pemmican to be cut off and given in little pieces back to us. It is ours and we will take what we want.[14]

Following an Indian Council meeting, the principal chiefs of Treaty Six, Mistawasis and Star Blanket, presented a list of demands to Commissioner Morris. He felt he had to respond as positively as he could or no treaty would be signed.

During Treaty Six negotiations, Morris responded to Indian demands for increased help for farming and health care assistance in the following way:

> You asked for help when you settled on your reserves during the time you were planting. You asked very broadly at first. I think the request you make now is reasonable to some extent; but help should be given after you settle on the reserve for three years only, for after that time you should have food of your own raising, besides all the things that are given to you; this assistance would only be given to those actually cultivating the soil. Therefore, I would agree to give every spring, for three years, the sum of one thousand dollars to assist you in buying provisions while planting the ground.[15]

In all the treaty negotiations, the Indians were promised that they would be taken care of by the Queen if they fulfilled their side of the bargain. For the chiefs, this relationship of mutual obligation was to endure "as long as the sun shines and the rivers flow." From the Indian point of view, the government failed to fulfill all of the promises in the years following the treaties.

The mutual, ongoing political and economic relationships spelled out at the time of the treaties are an essential part of the fabric of Canadian history. Further negotiation and resolution of continuing concerns are required.

Sharing Ideas

1. On what basis do lawyers today question the intent of treaties drawn up in the late 1800s?

2. What was: the British view of land transactions?
   the Indian view of land transactions?
   Why is this distinction crucial in understanding the present controversy over land in Canada?

3. In the land transfers, some Indian groups felt only agricultural lands would be used, but much which remained "precious" to their survival would remain untouched. List these areas which would be protected.

4. Treaty Six protects the essentials of Indian livelihood and survival. Briefly describe the concept of survival as it relates to the terms of Treaty Six.

5. How were reserve lands to be allotted to Indian peoples? What was the role of the government? What was the role of the Indian leaders?

6. Evaluate the differing view toward reserves between the British and the Indians.

Investigating Issues

1. "This is our land! It isn't just a piece of pemmican to be cut off and given in little pieces back to us. It is ours and we will take what we want." — Chief Poundmaker. Write a position paper using Chief Poundmaker's quote as the main theme. Did the Indians of Canada knowingly give up their land to the government? Support your view with two or three arguments you have studied.

2. Various Indian tribes had a different view of the implications of land use and transfer. Outline the perceptions of the:
   a) Plains Cree Indians, and
   b) Blackfoot tribes.

Key Words

Cede To give up, yield or surrender.

Compensation Payment or reimbursement for goods or services received.

Guardian One who is put in charge or in trust of a person or persons.

Integrate To unite with something else.

Oral accounts Historical events passed on by word of mouth.

Chapter 2
Northern Treaties
Treaty Eight Case Study

Are the terms good forever? As long as the sun shines on us? Because there are orphans we must consider, so that there will be nothing to be thrown up to us by our people afterwards. We want a written treaty, one copy to be given to us so we know what we sign for. Are you willing to give means to instruct children as long as the sun shines and water flows, so that our children will grow up ever increasing in knowledge?

— Kinosayoo, 1899

How were the northern tribes different from the prairie Indians?

The government entered into treaty negotiations on the prairies for several reasons. It wanted legal title to rich, fertile land for farming and settlement, as well as rights of way for the Canadian Pacific Railway. It also wanted to avoid the American government's costly experience of Indian wars. Once these goals were achieved, there were no further reasons, from the government's point of view, to extend the treaty-making process elsewhere in Canada.

It was not until 1899, twenty-two years after Treaty Seven, that the Indian tribes in northern Canada began treaty negotiations with the federal government. Agreements on Treaties Eight, Nine and Ten were made from 1899 to 1906. Treaty Eleven was signed in 1921.

We will use Treaty Eight as a case study because it set a pattern for the treaties that followed.

The Treaty Eight area extends from northern Saskatchewan, Alberta and British Columbia up to Great Slave Lake in the Northwest Territories.

The Athabascans, or Dene, had lived in northwestern Canada for centuries. Tribes included the Chipewyans, Beavers, Slaveys, Dogribs and Yellowknives.

Family units and small, loosely-organized bands moved around within flexible territories. This was in contrast to the larger, tightly-organized buffalo-hunting bands on the prairies. Northern band numbers were small compared to those of the prairie Indians.

By the early 1700s, the fur trade had moved into what is now northern Alberta. The geography and terrain of the area was ideally suited for trapping. The severe northern winters made physical survival more difficult. It also enhanced the quality and therefore the value of the furs.

Initially, the Woodland Cree were heavily involved in the fur trade. They had developed extensive networks with the European traders. They also used their

Life for the northern tribes was characterized by harsh climate, where they hunted, fished and trapped according to the season and availability of plants and animals.

strategic fur trade position to spread into areas that had been controlled by the Chipewyan.

The Cree traded furs for guns, and then forcefully moved into territories held by the Chipewyan and Beaver in the north. Later, the expansion of fur trading posts undercut the middlemen position of the Cree. By then, however, they had made inroads into the territory.

Both the Hudson's Bay Company and the Northwest Company were quick to recognize the rich fur trade potential of the Athabasca River system. Fort Chipewyan, established in 1788, is the oldest permanent settlement in Alberta. Both companies had a trading post there.

Trade networks, following the Peace and Athabasca River systems,

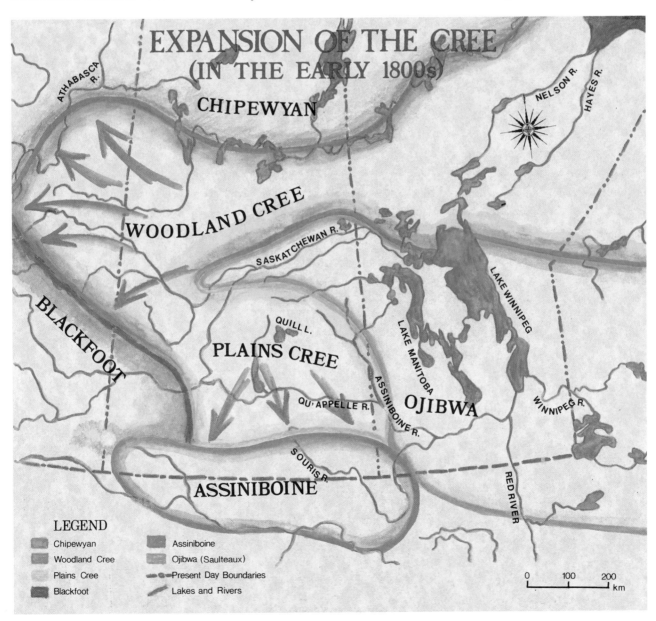

EXPANSION OF THE CREE
(IN THE EARLY 1800s)

CHIPEWYAN

ATHABASCA R.

NELSON R.

HAYES R.

WOODLAND CREE

SASKATCHEWAN R.

LAKE WINNIPEG

BLACKFOOT

QUILL L.

PLAINS CREE

QU'APPELLE R.

ASSINIBOINE R.

LAKE MANITOBA

OJIBWA

WINNIPEG R.

SOURIS R.

ASSINIBOINE

RED RIVER

LEGEND

▨ Chipewyan		▨ Assiniboine	
▨ Woodland Cree		▨ Ojibwa (Saulteaux)	
▨ Plains Cree		▬▬ Present Day Boundaries	
▨ Blackfoot		▬ Lakes and Rivers	

0   100   200
km

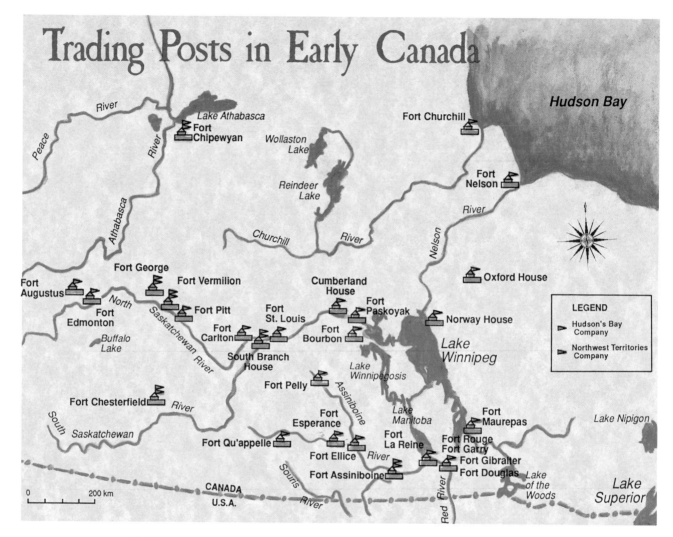

Trading Posts in Early Canada

Peace River

Athabasca River

Lake Athabasca

Fort Chipewyan

Wollaston Lake

Reindeer Lake

Churchill River

Fort Churchill

Hudson Bay

Fort Nelson

Nelson River

Oxford House

Fort George

Fort Vermilion

Cumberland House

Fort Paskoyak

Fort Augustus

North Saskatchewan River

Fort Edmonton

Fort Pitt

Fort St. Louis

Norway House

Buffalo Lake

Fort Carlton

Fort Bourbon

Lake Winnipeg

South Branch House

Lake Winnipegosis

Fort Pelly

Fort Chesterfield

River

Assiniboine River

Lake Manitoba

Fort Maurepas

Lake Nipigon

South Saskatchewan

Fort Esperance

Fort La Reine

Fort Rouge
Fort Garry

Fort Qu'appelle

Fort Ellice

River

Fort Gibralter
Fort Douglas

Lake of the Woods

Lake Superior

Souris River

Fort Assiniboine

Red River

CANADA
U.S.A.

0   200 km

LEGEND
- Hudson's Bay Company
- Northwest Territories Company

spread throughout the north. The fur traders were accepted by the Athabascan Indians as long as they adapted to the Indian ways by forming a reciprocal, or shared, relationship.

The fur trade was important to the livelihood of the northern tribes, just as it was to the prairie Indians. The Athabascan Indians benefited materially from the fur trade, but did not lose control over their culture or land and resources. Like the prairie Indians, the land remained the

source of their livelihood. They had no desire nor economic need to change their way of life. Over time, the Athabascan Indians adopted some technology and conveniences of the European trade goods.

The Metis population living in the north earned their living through traditional pursuits such as hunting, fishing and trapping. They also obtained seasonal wage labour in the transportation and fur trade systems.

The northern experience with newcomers was a mixed blessing.

Diseases, which northern Native peoples had no immunity to, devastated the Native population. Smallpox killed an estimated ninety percent of some Chipewyan bands.

After the 1821 merging of the fur trading companies, the Indians dealt exclusively with the Hudson's Bay Company.

Company practice by the 1860s provided for credit. A trapper could get supplies for the winter and bring in his furs for payment the next spring.

Also, the doctor attached to the trading post gave treatment to both the Indian and non-Native residents. Over the years, a cooperative relationship developed between the company and the northern tribes.

This relationship changed in 1870. The Hudson's Bay Company came to an agreement with the federal government. The company gave up its land rights in exchange for other benefits. The aboriginal inhabitants of the area then became the responsibility of the Government of Canada.

Although the fur trade continued, the Hudson's Bay Company was reluctant to provide aid to the Indians. The company believed that assistance should now be provided by the government.

Missionaries had begun entering the north by the 1860s. Another relationship of trust developed between the churches and the Indian peoples.

Missionaries wanted the federal government to provide for the Indians when the hunt was poor.

The Indians experienced hardships and starvation when resources were low. The missionaries wanted the government to provide a kind of "safety net" for the difficult times when the hunt was poor.

From 1870 to 1890, Vital Grandin, the Catholic Bishop at St. Albert, wrote many times to the Prime Minister of Canada "respecting the poor Indians . . . not yet looked after by the Government."

The federal government had limited sources of income during this period. It said it had no legal responsibility for Indians because treaties had not been signed in the northern area.

Missionaries, Hudson's Bay Company employees and Indian leaders continued to press the government for rations and supplies. By the late 1880s, public opinion seemed to run in favour of assistance for the Indians.

The years 1887 and 1888 were especially difficult for the northern tribes. Starvation was widespread among the Indians in the Treaty Eight area. The government did finally provide some relief assistance, channeled through the Hudson's Bay Company and the churches.

On January 1, 1890, a meeting of Indian representatives was held near Lesser Slave Lake. The leading chief of the Woodland Cree, Kinosayoo (or Keenooshayo), asked a friendly fur trader to tell the government that a large majority of Indians wanted to enter into treaty with the government. Apparently, Kinosayoo received "many letters written in Cree" from the Peace River area. The letters indicated a desire for treaty relations with the government.

However, the government at this point was not anxious to start with treaty negotiations.

Bishop Vital Grandin urged the government to help the northern Indian peoples.

Sharing Ideas

1. Explain how the following depended on each other:
   a) the Indians and the European traders,
   b) the trappers and the Hudson's Bay Company, and
   c) the Catholic and Anglican Churches and the Indians.

   Explain why these relationships developed.

2. Was the government willing to provide assistance to the Northern Indians? Why?

Investigating Issues

1. Using a chart similar to the one below, list the northern and prairie tribes, their living conditions and the trading patterns.

Tribe	Living Conditions	Relations with Traders

Key Words

Band The english name given to Indian clans and families by the Indian Act.

Reciprocal To return equally or in kind.

Why did the government finally negotiate Treaty Eight?

In the early 1880s, the government saw no reason to seek treaty relations in the north. The land was not yet needed for settlement and it was difficult to know if it might be needed in the future.

As well, the government was finding the prairie treaties more costly to carry out than expected. In fact, three-quarters of the spending of the Indian Affairs Department was related to prairie treaties. However, the prairie Indians were only one-quarter of the Canadian Indian population.

The Indian transition to agriculture was not going smoothly. The government feared the northern Indians would abandon their traditional way of life and become dependent on government provisions.

For a number of reasons, however, the government modified its position over a period of time.

Geological survey expeditions sent north in the 1880s reported that the territories might be more valuable than previously thought.

The petroleum potential of the Athabasca and MacKenzie valleys appeared to be enormous. This was at a time when the world demand for petroleum was expanding rapidly. Deposits of silver, copper, iron and other minerals were also found.

As well, the possibility of agriculture in some of the river valleys, particularly in the Peace River country, was reported.

At first, the government discouraged people from moving into the area because no northern treaties had been signed. However, improved transportation routes soon made access easier.

In 1880, a wagon road was completed from Edmonton to Athabasca Landing. By 1882, this road provided a link to steamboats on the Athabasca and MacKenzie river systems. Another road was built from the western end of Lesser

Steamships on the Athabasca and MacKenzie Rivers.

The discovery of gold in the Klondike in 1896 brought many prospectors through the northern area.

Slave Lake to the upper Peace River. These new transportation routes brought more non-Indian trappers and settlers into the north. The illegal use by some trappers of poison bait threatened the Indian way of life. They were also over-fishing Lesser Slave Lake and depleting the game along the overland routes. The invasion by prospectors resulted in clashes with local Indians:

> The gold seekers . . . plunged into the wilderness without hesitation, and without as much as 'by your leave' to the native. Some of these marauders, as was to be expected, exhibited a . . . contempt for the Indians' rights. At various places his horses were killed, his dogs shot, his bear traps broken up. An outcry arose in consequence, which inevitably would have led to reprisals and bloodshed had not the Government stepped in and forestalled further trouble by a prompt recognition of the native's title.[1]

A North West Mounted Police detachment was established at Athabasca Landing in 1892. From 1897 onwards, regular patrols were made into the north. The police force attempted to control the illegal liquor trade, eliminate the use of poison bait, enforce game laws and establish a degree of trust with the Indians. The NWMP feared increased conflict between the non-Native trappers and prospectors, and the Indians. The NWMP urged the federal government to sign a treaty with the Indians to establish law and order in the area.

In the end, it was the Klondike Gold Rush, and not the hardships experienced by the northern Indians, that prompted the government to begin treaty negotiations.

The government needed to keep a transportation corridor open through the north, and to maintain law and order in the territory. As well, with so many Americans moving through the area on their way to the Klondike, the government had to assert Canada's sovereignty in an area with few permanent, non-Native inhabitants.

The North West Mounted Police began making regular patrols into the north in 1897 to maintain law and order in the territory.

Sharing Ideas

1. What impact did the white trappers and settlers have on Treaty Eight?

2. List the reasons why the North West Mounted Police were stationed in the area.

3. Assess the impact the gold seekers had on Native communities.

4. Summarize the reasons why the government eventually felt it necessary to establish a treaty in the north.

Investigating Issues

1. Foreigners had a tremendous impact on the traditional Indian way of life. Examine the long-term implications of this exposure.

2. What factors, other than the gold rush, impacted on the Indian peoples of the north? Could these problems have been avoided by the government?

3. Did the northern treaties assist the Indian people to cope with developments in the north?

Key Words

Deplete To use up or run out of.

Marauder One who raids or loots.

Reprisal Retaliation against another.

Did each side get what they wanted from the treaties?

By 1898, the Government of Canada was finally ready to negotiate treaties with the northern tribes.

The area to be covered by Treaty Eight was the area north of Treaty Six. This area was needed for mining, farming and transportation routes.

Notices of meetings for the following year were distributed by the NWMP and the missionaries. They tried to answer questions from the Indians about the government's plans.

Through those discussions, the government received information that the Indians might refuse the treaty. The Indians feared that settlement of their land would interfere with their way of life. Also, the northern tribes did not want to settle on reserves as the prairie tribes had done.

The federal government had decided to hold negotiations with the Indians and Metis at the same time. The government thought that the Metis might disrupt negotiations if they felt their claims were being neglected. Metis claims were to be handled by a Scrip Commission.

The Treaty Eight commissioners were David Laird, J. H. Ross and D. A. J. McKenna. The Scrip commissioners were J. Arthur Cote and James Walker.

The Scrip Commission had authority to issue land scrip, or tokens, for 240 acres, or money

Metis land scrip entitled the owner to 240 acres of Dominion lands for homesteading.

scrip worth $240.00. Most Metis chose money scrip. There were 1 243 scrip issued at Lesser Slave Lake, Peace River, Fort Vermilion and Fort Chipewyan.

The numbers of scrip issued indicates there were enough Metis to be significant to both the government and Indian representatives at the treaty negotiations. In comparison, a total of 2 217 Indians were paid treaty money in 1899, and a further 1 218 Indians joined the treaty in 1900.

Another important point is that Metis who were living as Indians and accepted within their bands had the option of taking treaty rights instead of scrip.

The head commissioner for Treaty Eight, David Laird, was expected to follow the terms of the earlier treaties. However, he was given a certain amount of power by the government to negotiate additional terms, provided he kept cost considerations in mind.

A new concept found in Treaty Eight was the allowance for small family reserves. These were referred to as reserves in severalty. This meant that the reserves were created for individual families. The government wanted to meet the

At Treaty Eight negotiations at Lesser Slave Lake, Commissioner Laird said the treaty would not take away the tribe's freedom to hunt, fish and trap.

Headman Moostoos and Chief Kinosayoo were two of the leading Cree spokesmen at Treaty Eight negotiations.

As with other treaty negotiations in the west, there were discussions among Indians prior to the treaty.

The Lesser Slave Lake Cree talked with the Cree in the Edmonton area prior to negotiations. They seemed to be aware of some of the problems involved with being confined to reserves. All the northern tribes remained suspicious of government assurances and promises.

Both the government and the Indians had done their homework for these negotiations. However, neither party could predict the changes to northern areas if development by non-Natives occurred quickly.

Treaty Eight negotiations in 1898 at Lesser Slave Lake began with the usual opening ceremonies and the appropriate symbolism and greetings.

The Queen's offer to Indian leaders was then made by Commissioner Laird. He stressed that the treaty would not take away the tribe's freedom to hunt, fish and trap. Laird said the treaty would confirm this right.

In reply, Chief Kinosayoo, asserted the right to negotiate additional treaty terms. He emphasized the need for freedom to make a living. The other leading Cree spokesman, Moostoos, supported Kinosayoo. Moostoos

needs of the family and small band groupings of the Dene and Woodland Cree.

The federal minister responsible for the treaty, Clifford Sifton, asked Father Albert Lacombe and other missionaries to reassure the Indians that their traditional way of life would not be harmed by the treaty.

stressed the need for peaceful relations between Indian peoples and the government.

Commissioner Ross then provided the initial government response to Chief Kinosayoo:

> [Kinosayoo] has said that he cannot see how it will benefit you to take treaty. As all the rights you now have will not be interfered with, therefore anything you get in addition must be clear gain. The white man is bound to come in and open up the country, and we come before him to explain the relations that must exist between you and thus preventing trouble.[2]

Later in the negotiations, Kinosayoo felt that some of his band members were doubtful. He then pressed for the educational needs of Indian children. He also questioned the long-term nature of treaty promises.

Kinosayoo sensed that the negotiations were moving towards a decision. He was anxious that the government not forget items which should be included:

> Are the terms good forever? As long as the sun shines on us? Because there are orphans we must consider, so that there will be nothing to be thrown up to us by our people afterwards. We want a written treaty, one copy to be given to us so we know what we sign for. Are you willing to give means to instruct children as long as the sun shines and water flows, so that our children will grow up ever increasing in knowledge?[3]

Laird indicated that he was prepared to include Kinosayoo's terms in order to conclude Treaty Eight negotiations:

> The government will choose teachers according to the religion of the band.... About the treaties lasting forever, I will just say that some Indians have got to live so like whites that they have sold their lands and divided the money. But this only happens when the Indians ask for it. Treaties will last forever as signed, unless the Indians wish to make a change. I understand you all agree to the terms of the treaty. Am I right? If so, I will have the treaty drawn up and tomorrow we will sign it. Speak all those who do not agree![4]

Many of the Cree Indians were still not satisfied. The government asked Father Lacombe to assure the Indians that the government's word could be accepted. He told them their way of life would not be changed by the treaty. Father Lacombe said that they would receive annuities, or yearly payments, for "as long as the sun shines and the earth remains."

After these guarantees from someone they trusted, the chiefs and counsellors stood up and urged others to do so. This signified their acceptance of the government offer.

When the terms of the treaty were read by the commissioners the following day, many young Indians remained skeptical. Further discussions were required before the treaty was signed. In their report, the Treaty Eight Commissioners recorded the nature of the suspicions:

> Our chief difficulty was the apprehension that the hunting and fishing privileges were to be curtailed. The provision in the treaty under which ammunition and twine is to be

furnished went far in the direction of quieting the fears of the Indians, for they admitted that it would be unreasonable to furnish the means of hunting and fishing so restricted as to render it impossible to make a living by such pursuits.[5]

Laird, Ross and McKenna decided that the Lesser Slave Lake treaty text should constitute Treaty Eight. They travelled to other tribes

Father Lacombe, who was trusted by the Indians, acted as a middleman between the parties during the treaty negotiations.

along the Peace and Athabasca River systems to get adhesions, or agreements, to the same terms. They obtained adhesions from Indian tribes at Peace River, Vermilion, Fort Chipewyan, Fond du Lac, Fort McMurray and Wabasca.

The following year, 1891, Commissioner McKenna took adhesions from Indian representatives at Fort St. John, and from a large number of Yellowknives, Dogribs and Chipewyans at Fort Resolution on Great Slave Lake.

Several important issues came up during the adhesion process that were recorded in the Commissioner's Report.

One of these issues was medical care. A young physician accompanied the commissioners. He treated the medical problems of the Indians gathered for the treaty negotiations. This may have prompted demands by chiefs for continued medical care. The commissioners' report acknowledged the earnest appeals for the services of a medical man.

The commissioners promised that free medical supplies would be given to any Indians who needed them. These supplies would be located at certain points and would be provided by someone recommended by the government.

Some of the crucial aspects of Treaty Eight from the Indian perspective included:
1. the right to roam freely over the land and to continue hunting, fishing and trapping;

2. education for their children and for future generations;
3. free medical care; and
4. the promise of the commissioners that the treaties would last forever.

The economic measures demanded by the prairie Indians to help them in their transition to farming would be made available to the northern Indians once they settled on reserves.

The government's objectives seem to have been accomplished. These included acquiring clear title to the land and mineral resources, as well as peaceful relations with the Indian bands.

The stories and accounts of negotiations for the other northern treaties are important in their own right, but will not be covered here. There were, however, similar themes in Treaties Nine, Ten and Eleven.

Hunting, fishing and trapping continued to be very important for the northern Indian tribes. In their negotiations, the government's main concerns involved acquiring land and resources, and peaceful relations.

There were, however, certain differences. For example, the Indian tribes in the Treaty Nine area wanted to have actual reserve locations included in their treaty. The province of Ontario was also involved in Treaty Nine negotiations.

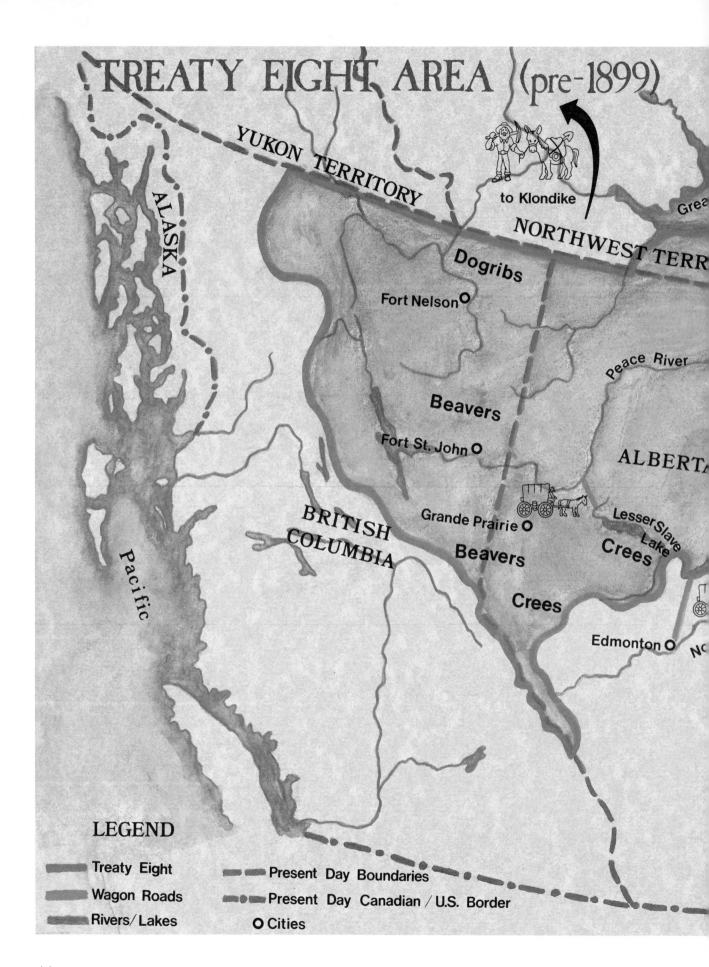

TREATY EIGHT AREA (pre-1899)

to Klondike

YUKON TERRITORY

NORTHWEST TERR

ALASKA

Dogribs

Fort Nelson O

Great

Peace River

Beavers

Fort St. John O

ALBERTA

BRITISH
COLUMBIA

Grande Prairie O

Lesser Slave
Lake

Beavers

Crees

Pacific

Crees

Edmonton O   No

LEGEND

▬▬▬	Treaty Eight	▬ ▬ ▬	Present Day Boundaries
▬▬▬	Wagon Roads	▬·▬·▬	Present Day Canadian / U.S. Border
▬▬▬	Rivers/Lakes	O	Cities

Timeline of Treaties and Northern Expansion

Prior to 1788   Chipewyan, Beaver, Slave and Cree Nations occupy Treaty Eight area.

1788   Hudson's Bay Company establishes post at Fort Chipewyan.

1821   Hudson's Bay Company and North West Company amalgamate.

1857   Palliser and Hind expeditions.

1860   Missionaries begin entering the north.

1870   Hudson's Bay Company relinquishes title to Rupert's Land. Manitoba joins Confederation.

1871   British Columbia joins Confederation.

1871 to 1877   Treaties One to Seven signed.

1880   Wagon road completed from Edmonton to Athabasca Landing.

1880s   Northern Indians petition government for treaties. Government sends survey expeditions north.

1892   North West Mounted Police post established at Athabasca Landing.

1896   Klondike Gold Rush.

1899   Treaty Eight signed.

1900   Adhesions obtained to Treaty Eight.

1905   Alberta and Saskatchewan join Confederation. Treaty Nine signed.

1906   Treaty Ten signed.

1921   Treaty Eleven signed.

Sharing Ideas

1. For what reasons were the Indians initially hesitant to sign a treaty with the government of Canada?

2. Describe the geographic area of Treaty Eight and explain the significance of the area.

3. Explain the two options the Metis had when dealing with the commissioners.

4. Identify the following people and the role they played in the negotiations of Treaty Eight:
   a) David Laird,
   b) Father Lacombe,
   c) Chief Kinosayoo,
   d) Moostoos,
   e) Commissioner Ross, and
   f) Commissioner McKenna.

5. Summarize the results of Treaty Eight for:
   a) the Indian people, and
   b) the Government of Canada.

Investigating Issues

1. Why do some people today question the extent of the assurances of Treaty Eight?

2. Compare the written text of Treaty Eight with the Commissioner's Report, dated September 22, 1899. Were there possible misunderstandings in terms of medical treatment, and hunting, fishing and trapping rights?

Key Words

Adhesion Agreement or consent to an existing agreement.

Annuity A sum of money payable yearly.

Confirm To assure the validity of something or to remove doubt by an authoritative act.

Reserves in severalty Reserves for small families.

Scrip A certificate which entitles the holder or bearer to land or money.

Symbolism The use of something that stands for or represents something else.

Chapter 3
Historical Overview

The mountains were not even mentioned, according to my grandfather, because they would not be useful, and 'anything that cannot be used agriculturally will be yours.' He did not understand how the white man came to own the timber and the minerals and the animals.

– Elder John Buffalo, 1975

How did each side understand the treaties?

The Indian and government negotiators had different goals when negotiating the treaties.

The Indian negotiators had the following set of goals:

1. To ensure the physical survival of Indian nations;
2. To keep peaceful relations with the Canadian government through ongoing relationships of equality and respect;
3. To affirm the ongoing cultural and spiritual survival as distinct Indian tribes and nations, by preserving distinctive traditions and institutions; and
4. To be able to make a transition to a new lifestyle by borrowing certain technologies, including the treaty promises involving educational, economic, health and other benefits.

Following are the main goals of the federal government:

1. To acquire legal title to western and northern lands for farming, railways, mining and other types of development;
2. To peacefully settle the west with Ontario and European immigrant farmers;
3. To keep the costs of this westward expansion at a minimum, and in particular to avoid costly wars with Indian and Metis inhabitants;
4. To stop American expansion into Canada's western and northern territories, and to protect these territories; and
5. To respond, to some degree, to Indian requests for treaties and treaty benefits.

In many ways, it is remarkable that Treaties One to Eleven were finally settled and signed. Different perceptions by the Indian peoples and the federal government, often based on different cultural, social and economic viewpoints, continue today. There are, however, real areas of agreement to be found in the written treaty promises.

One area of misunderstanding in treaty negotiations concerned land and resources which were not set aside for reserves, and not required by the incoming settlers for farming.

...ans wanted to have the opportunity to take on a ...ifestyle by borrowing certain technology.

The government wanted to peacefully settle the west.

The following statement, taken in the mid-1970s, from an Indian elder, illustrates this problem:

> This is the story they always related to us, the manner by which the chief was dealt with. He would indicate with his hands approximately one foot in depth. 'That is the depth that is requested from you, that is what the deal is, nothing below the surface, that will always belong to you. Only land where agriculture can be viable; other areas where nothing can grow, that will always belong to you. You will always be owner of that land.' That is what they were promised. That is why they were agreeable to the treaty because the promises were so good . . . the mountains were not even mentioned, according to my grandfather, because they would not be useful, and 'anything that cannot be used agriculturally will be yours.' He did not understand how the white man came to own the timber and the minerals and the animals.[1]

The spoken words of the commissioners during treaty negotiations were much more important to the Indian representatives than the written document.

The Indian leaders were aware of the need for a record of the agreement.

Traditionally, this involved understanding what was said and memorizing it. This, in turn, was orally passed on to those who did not attend the negotiations and to successive generations.

From 1867 to 1869, S. J. Dawson, the Dominion surveyor, warned his superiors in Ottawa prior to Treaty One negotiations, that Indian culture respects and emphasizes oral history:

> At these gatherings it is necessary to observe extreme caution in what is said, as, though they have no means of writing, there are always those present who are charged to keep every word in mind. As an instance of the manner in which records are in this way kept, without writing, I may mention that, on one occasion, at Fort Frances, the principal chief of the tribe commenced an oration, by repeating, almost [word for word], what I had said to him two years previously. For my own part, I would have the fullest reliance as to these Indians observing a treaty and adhering most strictly to all its provisions, if, in the first place it were concluded after *full discussion and after all its provisions were thoroughly understood by the Indians*, and if, in the next, it were never infringed upon by the whites, who are generally the first to break [the] Indian treaties.[2]

Indian negotiators' main concern was the current and future well-being of their people. They demanded larger reserves, agricultural aid, hunting supplies and medical treatment.

While Commissioner Morris did his best to negotiate treaty terms which carried out the government's instructions, or mandate, he also responded to Indian demands for more favourable terms. The government felt Morris went too far in Treaty Six negotiations. He agreed to Indian requests for medical supplies, and additional farming supplies and grain. He also agreed to a famine and epidemic relief clause. These promises were insisted on by the Indian negotiators. To get Indian agreement, the commissioners were forced to make changes in the treaties.

> Credit must be given to the treaty Commissioners, who showed some understanding of the problem and exercised enough flexibility to meet Indian suggestions part way.[3]

Each subsequent treaty tended to build on terms that had already been negotiated in earlier treaties and new demands were often made.

Today, Indian people take the view that rights obtained in any treaty apply to all treaty Indians. They view the treaty process as a "bundle of rights" which apply equally to all Indian peoples.

The long-term physical and cultural survival of Indian nations were key elements that Indian negotiators believed were included in the treaties.

Similarly, the government reached its objective of peacefully opening up the Canadian west and north for farm settlement and mining.

Summary of Canada's Treaties with the Indians of Manitoba and the Northwest Territories

1. A relinquishment (giving up), in all the great region from Lake Superior to the foot of the Rocky Mountains, of all their right and title to the lands covered by the treaties, saving certain reservations for their own use, and

2. In return for such relinquishment, permission to the Indians to hunt over the ceded (released) territory and to fish in the waters thereof, excepting such portions of the territory as pass from the Crown into the occupation of individuals or otherwise.

3. The perpetual (never-ending) payment of annuities of five dollars per head to each Indian – man, woman and child. The payment of an annual salary of twenty-five dollars to each chief, and of fifteen dollars to each councillor, or head man, of a chief (thus making them in a sense officers of the Crown), and in addition, suits of official clothing for the chiefs and head men, British flags for the chiefs, and silver medals.

4. The allotment of lands to the Indians, to be set aside as reserves for them for homes and agricultural purposes, and which cannot be sold or

Queen Victoria was the ruling monarch for most of the treaties.

alienated without their consent, and then only for their benefit; the extent of lands thus set apart being generally one section for each family of five.

5. A very important feature of all the treaties, is the giving to the Indian bands, agricultural implements, oxen, cattle (to form the nuclei of herds), and seed grain.

6. The treaties provide for the establishment of schools, on the reserves, for the instruction of the Indian children.

7. The treaties all provide for the exclusion of the sale of spirits, or [alcohol], on the reserves.

Such are the main features of the treaties between Canada and the Indians, and, few as they are, they comprehend the whole future of the Indians and of their relations to the Dominion.[4]

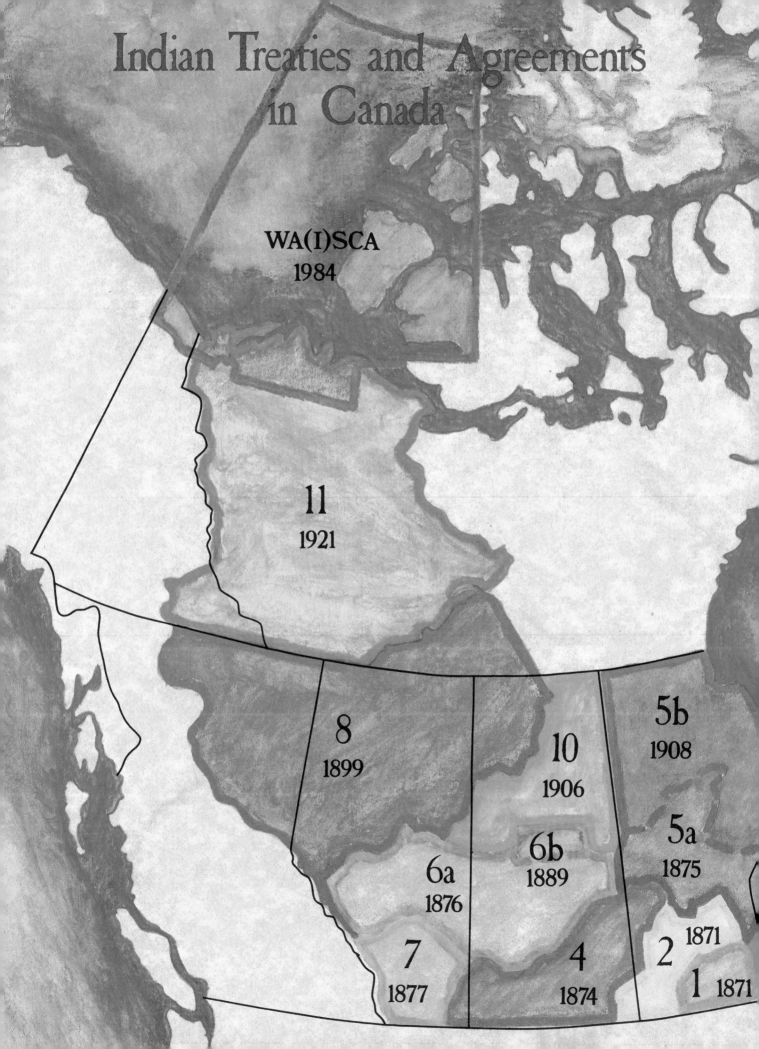

Indian Treaties and Agreements in Canada

WA(I)SCA
1984

11
1921

8
1899

10
1906

5b
1908

6b
1889

5a
1875

6a
1876

7
1877

4
1874

2 1871

1 1871

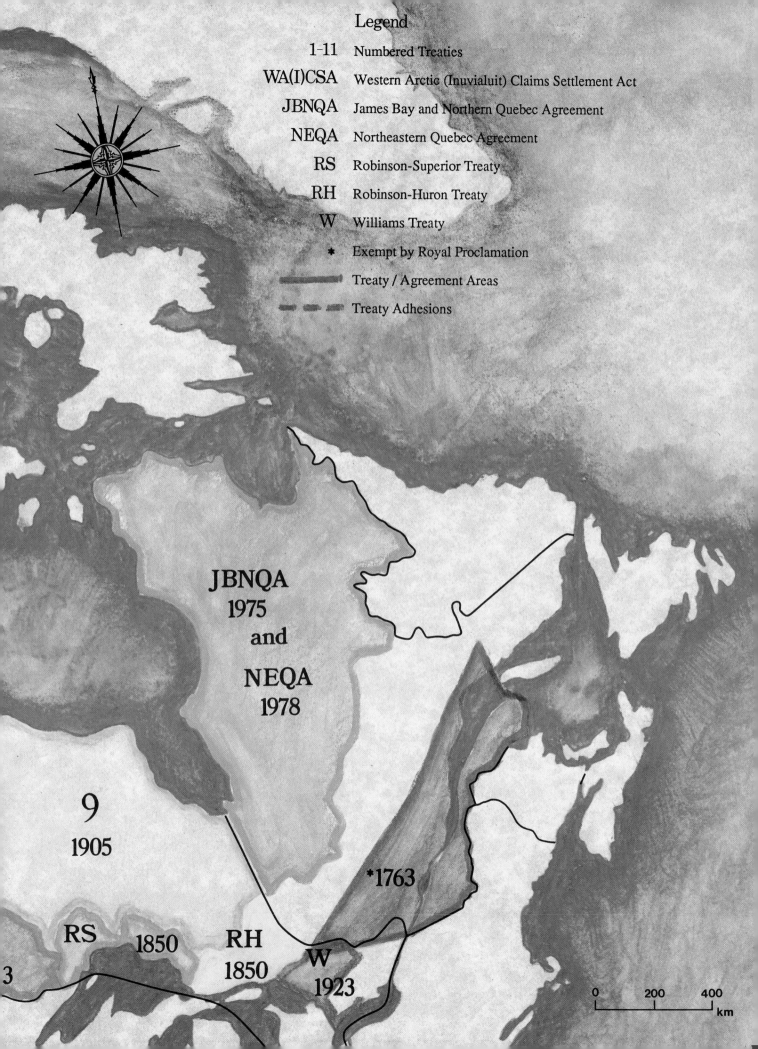

Legend

1-11	Numbered Treaties
WA(I)CSA	Western Arctic (Inuvialuit) Claims Settlement Act
JBNQA	James Bay and Northern Quebec Agreement
NEQA	Northeastern Quebec Agreement
RS	Robinson-Superior Treaty
RH	Robinson-Huron Treaty
W	Williams Treaty
*	Exempt by Royal Proclamation
———	Treaty / Agreement Areas
- - -	Treaty Adhesions

JBNQA
1975
and
NEQA
1978

9
1905

*1763

RS   RH
3   1850   1850   W
1923

0   200   400
km

WRITTEN TREATY PROMISES — TREATIES ONE TO FIVE

	PEACE AND GOODWILL	HEALTH	EDUCATION	HUNTING, FISHING AND TRAPPING
TREATY ONE 1871	• Mutual obligations.	• Not mentioned in written treaty text.	• Maintain a school on each reserve at the Indians' request.	• Not mentioned in written treaty text.
TREATY TWO 1871	• Mutual obligations.	• Not mentioned in written treaty text.	• Maintain a school on each reserve at the Indians' request.	• Not mentioned in written treaty text.
TREATY THREE 1873	• Mutual obligations.	• Not mentioned in written treaty text.	• Maintain schools for instruction where requested by Indian bands.	• Pursue avocations of hunting and fishing throughout the surrendered area, except on land taken up for settlement, mining, lumbering or other purposes by the government and subject to regulations of the government. • The government to spend $1 500 a year on ammunition and twine (for nets).
TREATY FOUR 1874	• Mutual obligations.	• Not mentioned in written treaty text.	• Maintain a school on a reserve as soon as a band is settled and is prepared for a teacher.	• Pursue avocations of hunting and fishing throughout the surrendered area, except on land taken up for settlement, mining, lumbering or other purposes by the government and subject to regulations of the government. • The government to spend $750 a year on powder, shot, bale and twine.
TREATY FIVE 1875	• Mutual obligations.	• Not mentioned in written treaty text.	• Maintain schools for instruction on reserves when the federal government deems it advisable and Indians desire schools.	• Pursue avocations of hunting and fishing throughout the surrendered area, except on land taken up for settlement, mining, lumbering or other purposes by the government and subject to regulations of the government. • The government to spend $300 a year on ammunition and twine.

Please Note: The descriptions of the promises of the treaties are those found in the written treaty text. Indian oral traditions regarding treaty promises often include more extensive understandings of the spirit and intent of treaty promises. Indian peoples also view these treaty rights as applying to all treaty Indians. For example, the Treaty Six Medicine Chest, symbolized today by medical care rights, should apply to all Indians living within other treaty areas.

LAND	FARMING ASSISTANCE	PAYMENTS, ANNUITIES AND SPECIAL BENEFITS
• Reserves of one-quarter section (160 acres) for each family of five.	• Per family: A plow and a harrow for each settler cultivating the ground. A boar and a sow for each family prepared to receive them. • Per chief: A bull and a cow. A boar and a sow. A plough and a harrow.	• Per Indian person: $5.00 per year. Payment could be taken in clothing or equipment. • Per chief: $20.00 per year. A buggy. A suit of clothing every three years. • Per headman (Four per band): A suit of clothing every three years.
• Reserves of one-quarter section (160 acres) for each family of five.	• Per family: A plow and a harrow for each settler cultivating the ground. A boar and a sow for each family prepared to receive them. • Per chief: A bull and a cow. A boar and a sow. A plough and a harrow.	• Per Indian person: $5.00 per year. Payment could be taken in clothing or equipment. • Per chief: $20.00 per year. A buggy. A suit of clothing every three years. • Per headman (Four per band): A suit of clothing every three years.
• Reserves of one section (640 acres) for each family of five.	• Per family: Two hoes, one spade, one scythe. • Per ten families: One plough. • Per twenty families: Five harrows. • Per band: one axe, one cross-cut saw, one handsaw, one pit-saw, one grindstone, one auger, enough wheat, barley and potatoes to plant the cultivated land, and one yoke of oxen, one bull and four cows.	• Per Indian person: $12.00 at treaty signing. • Per chief: $25.00 annual salary. A medal and a flag. A suit of clothing every three years. • Per headman (Five only): $15.00 annual salary. A suit of clothing every three years.
• Reserve land of one section (640 acres) for each family of five.	• Per family: Two hoes, one spade, one scythe, one axe for every family cultivating the soil. Enough seed (wheat, barley, oats and potatoes) to plant such land actually broken up. • Per ten families: One plough and one harrow. • Per chief: One yoke of oxen, one bull, four cows, a chest of ordinary carpenter's tools, five hand saws, four augers, one cross-cut saw, one pit saw, the necessary files and one grindstone.	• Per Indian person: $5.00 annually. Gift of clothing. • Per chief: $25.00 gift and $25.00 annually. A coat and a Queen's silver medal. A suit of clothing every three years. • Per headman (Four per band): $15.00 gift and $15.00 annually. A suit of clothing every three years.
• Reserve land of one-quarter section (160 acres) for each family of five. • Reserves may be sold by the government with consent of and for benefit of said Indians or appropriated by government with due compensation.	• Per family: Two hoes, one axe, one scythe and one spade for families cultivating land. • Per ten families: One plough. • Per twenty families: Five harrows. • Per chief: One cross-cut saw, one pit saw, the necessary files, one grindstone and one auger. Enough wheat, barley, potatoes and oats to plant land cultivated. One yoke of oxen, one bull and four cows.	• Per Indian person: $5.00 payment at treaty signing and $5.00 annually. • Per chief: $25.00 gift and $25.00 annually. A coat and a Queen's silver medal. A suit of clothing every three years. • Per headman (Three per band): $15.00 gift and $15.00 annually. A suit of clothing every three years.

WRITTEN TREATY PROMISES — TREATIES SIX TO ELEVEN

	PEACE AND GOODWILL	HEALTH	EDUCATION	HUNTING, FISHING AND TRAPPING
TREATY SIX 1876	• Mutual obligations.	• Medicine chest to be kept at home of Indian Agent for the use and benefits of the Indians. • Assistance as deemed necessary and sufficient for relief in event of famine or pestilence.	• Maintenance of schools on reserves.	• Pursue avocations of hunting and fishing throughout the surrendered area, except on land taken up for settlement, mining, lumbering or other purposes by the government and subject to regulations of the government. • The government to spend $1 500 a year on ammunition and twine.
TREATY SEVEN 1877	• Mutual obligations.	• Not mentioned in written treaty text.	• Salary for teacher for children once Indians settled on reserves.	• Right to pursue the avocations of hunting and fishing throughout the surrendered area, except on land taken up for settlement, mining, lumbering or other purposes by the government and subject to regulations of the government. • The government to spend $2000 a year on ammunition.
TREATY EIGHT 1899	• Mutual obligations.	• Mentioned in Commissioner's Report, but not mentioned in written treaty text.	• Salaries for teachers.	• Right to pursue vocations of hunting, fishing and trapping throughout the surrendered area, except on land taken up for settlement, mining, lumbering, trading or other purposes by the government and subject to regulations of the government. • Ammunition and twine at a value of $1 per head of families engaged in hunting and fishing.
TREATY NINE 1905 and 1906	• Mutual obligations.	• Not mentioned in written treaty text.	• Federal government agrees to pay salaries of teachers and to provide school buildings and educational equipment (as government deems advisable).	• Right to pursue vocations of hunting, fishing and trapping throughout the surrendered area, except on land taken up for settlement, mining, lumbering, trading or other purposes by the government and subject to regulations of the government. • Ammunition and twine at a value of $1 per head of families engaged in hunting and fishing.
TREATY TEN 1906 **TREATY ELEVEN 1921**	• Mutual obligations.	Mentioned in Commissioner's Report, but not mentioned in written treaty text.	• Federal government to make provision for the education of Indian children.	• Right to pursue vocations of hunting, fishing and trapping throughout the surrendered area, except on land taken up for settlement, mining, lumbering, trading or other purposes by the government and subject to regulations of the government. • Federal government agrees to make such a distribution of twine and ammunition to them annually as is usually made to Indians similarly situated.

Please Note: The descriptions of the promises of the treaties are those found in the written treaty text. Indian oral traditions regarding treaty promises often include more extensive understandings of the spirit and intent of treaty promises. Indian peoples also view these treaty rights as applying to all treaty Indians. For example, the Treaty Six Medicine Chest, symbolized today by medical care rights, should apply to all Indians living within other treaty areas.

LAND	FARMING ASSISTANCE	PAYMENTS, ANNUITIES AND SPECIAL BENEFITS
• Reserves of one square mile per family of five. • Reserves may be sold by the government with consent of and for benefit of said Indians or appropriated by government with due compensation.	• Per family: 4 hoes, 2 spades, 2 scythes, 1 wetstone, 2 hay forks, 2 reaping hooks and 2 axes. • Per three families: 1 plough and 1 harrow. • Per band: 1 cross-cut saw, 1 handsaw, 1 pit-saw, the necessary files, 1 grindstone, and 1 auger. Enough wheat, barley, potatoes and oats to plant broken land, plus 1 handmill when warranted, 4 oxen, 1 bull, 6 cows, 1 boar, 2 sows, 1 chest of carpenter's tools. All of the above to be given one sum at the discretion of Indian Agent and not exceeding $1000 to be used during three-year period to purchase provisions as incentive for band members actually engaged in cultivation.	• Per Indian person: $12.00 at treaty signing and $5.00 per year. • Per chief: One horse, one harness, and one wagon or two carts.
• Reserves of one square mile per family of five. • Reserves retain right to navigate the rivers and use the trails, and build to roads and bridges as necessary.	• Per family of ten or more: 4 cows. • Per family of five to ten: 3 cows. • Per family of five or less: 2 cows. • Per family: 2 hoes, 1 spade, 1 scythe and 2 hay forks. • Per three families: 1 plough and 1 harrow. • Per chief, minor chief and head for use of band: 1 bull or 1 cow. • Per band: Potatoes, barley, oats and wheat to plant on broken land.	• Per Indian person: $12.00 at treaty signing and $5.00 per year. • Per chief: $25.00 annually. • Per head chief, minor chief and councillor: A medal and a flag. A rifle the following year. A suit of clothing every three years. Per councillor: $15.00 annually.
• Reserves of one square mile per family of five or land in severalty of 160 acres per Indian. • Reserves may be sold by the government with consent of and for benefit of Indians. • Reserve land may be appropriated by the government with due compensation.	When settled: • Per family: 2 hoes, 1 spade, 1 scythe and 2 hay forks, and 1 cow. • Per three families: 1 plough and 1 harrow. • Per chief for use of band: 2 horses or yoke of oxen, 1 bull, 1 mowing machine, and 1 reaper. • Per band: Potatoes, barley, oats and wheat to plant on broken land, plus provisions for one month in spring during planting. For families preferring to raise stock instead of cultivating: • Per family of five: 2 cows. • Per chief: 2 bulls and 2 mowing machines.	• Per Indian person: $12.00 at treaty signing and $5.00 per year. • Per chief: $32.00 at time of treaty signing and $25.00 annually. One medal and one flag. A suit of clothing every three years. • Per headman: $22.00 at time of signing and $15.00 annually. A suit of clothing every three years.
• Reserves of one section (640 acres or one square mile) per family of five or land in severalty of 160 acres per Indian.	• Not mentioned.	• Per Indian person: $8.00 annually. • Per Indian head of family: $4.00 annually. • Per chief: $32.00. $8.00 payment. A flag and a copy of the treaty.
• Reserves of one section (640 acres or one square mile) per family of five or land in severalty of 160 acres per Indian. • Family reserves (reserve land in severalty): 160 acres per Indian family member.	• Federal government agrees to furnish such assistance as may be found necessary or advisable to aid and assist Indians in agriculture or in raising stock or other work.	• Per Indian person: $12.00 payment and $5.00 annually. • Per chief: $32.00 payment and $15.00 annually. Silver medal and flag for signing treaty. Suitable suit of clothing every three years. • Per headman: $22.00 payment and $15.00 annually. A bronze medal. A suit of clothing every three years.

Sharing Ideas

1. What were the goals of the Indian and government negotiators in the discussions leading up to the treaties?

2. Describe the main aspects of the treaties dealing with land, hunting, annuities, reservations, agriculture, education and alcohol.

Investigating Issues

1. In his book, *Skyscrapers Hide the Heavens*, (University of Toronto Press, 1989), J. R. Miller describes the treaty agreements as a "neat blend" of Indian and government sets of interests. Do you agree with this assessment?

2. Compare the written terms of three treaties. Outline some of the differences and similarities between these treaties. What factors may have influenced changes made in the treaties?

3. Research the geographic areas covered by Treaties One to Eleven and indicate them on a current map of Canada.

4. Make a timeline using the dates of the treaties. List the significant dates and events of Canadian exploration and settlement opposite the dates. Identify the concerns that influenced the dates and contents of the various treaties.

Key Words

Famine An extreme scarcity of food leading to widespread starvation.

Mandate An authorization given to a representative to do something.

Perpetual Continuing forever.

Relinquishment To give up or pass over.

Did the Indian treaties turn out the way the negotiators expected?

By 1879, the situation for the prairie Treaty Indians was critical. The buffalo herds had disappeared from the Canadian prairies. Only a few small herds were left in Montana.

There was little effort by the government to survey Indian reserves. As well, there was little attempt to assist in the Indian transition to agriculture. Rations were, however, provided to relieve problems of starvation among the buffalo-hunting tribes.

By the end of the 1870s, the government had provided few financial or human resources to put the treaty terms into effect. The next five years were characterized by severe financial restraint in government. Indian representatives felt the government had turned a deaf ear to their pleas for treaty implementation.

When Governor General Lorne visited western Canada in 1881, the Indian leaders protested the mishandling of their treaties.

Some chiefs, especially Cree Chief Big Bear and his followers, had refused to sign Treaty Six in 1876. They had not received strong

With the destruction of the buffalo herds, many Indian tribes were facing starvation.

camp would receive government rations:

> They are literally in a starving condition and destitute of the commonest necessaries of life. The disappearance of the Buffalo has left them not only without food, but also without Robes, mocassins (sic) and adequate Tents or Teppees . . . Their clothing for the most part was miserable and scanty in the extreme. I saw little children at this inclement season, snow having fallen, who had scarcely rags to cover them. Of food they possessed little or none . . .[5]

By the early 1880s, the Saskatchewan Cree people began a movement to seek treaty revisions. They felt the principles and spirit of the new Indian treaties were not being implemented. Agricultural supplies and farm animals arrived late and were often of poor quality. Some chiefs were prevented from choosing reserves adjacent to one another in the Cypress Hills.

A number of Indian councils were held to discuss the government's failure to live up to its side of the bargain. These councils came to a climax in a meeting in 1884 at Duck Lake, Saskatchewan. Twelve bands were represented. Cree Chiefs Piapot, Big Bear and Little Pike tried to rally a united front to force revisions to the treaties. Their efforts failed when the Metis resistance of 1885 brought the full force of the government army against the Metis and some Indian bands in Saskatchewan and Alberta.

It was not until after 1885 that the federal government provided more resources to carry out treaty

In 1882, Chief Big Bear was forced to sign Treaty Six to get government food rations.

assurance that a non-Indian legal and cultural system would not be imposed. Their fears seemed to be confirmed.

Chief Big Bear finally did adhere to Treaty Six in 1882 so that his

agreements. Even then, the government gave only what it considered necessary from its own narrow, legal and cost-conscious perspective.

Federal political parties were extremely aware of the cost of implementing the treaties. Treaty Commissioner Laird claimed in 1905 that the annual expenditures for Indians in Manitoba and the Northwest Territories during the last 20 years averaged over $730 000.

The extra promises in the treaties cost the government far more than they had ever expected, in spite of how slowly and incompletely the promises were fulfilled.

The government began to move away from the treaty promises in agreements it signed with other governments.

For example, the Treaty on Migratory Birds in 1916 between Canada, the United States and Mexico, put restrictions on Indian hunting rights.

Another agreement between Canada and the prairie provinces in 1930 required provincial agreement in selection of reserve land. The Natural Resources Transfer Agreements put further restrictions on hunting, fishing and trapping rights.

For Indian leaders, reserves represented a secure home base. It was a place where the Indian people could learn a new, self-supporting way of life. They would also continue to hunt, fish and trap. These Indian homelands were to be a means of ensuring the physical, cultural and spiritual survival of their people.

The federal government, on the other hand, saw the reserves as a "training ground." Reserves were meant to prepare the Indian people for citizenship in the Canadian culture and society. From the government's perspective, the reserves were to be a temporary residence until the Indian was "civilized," and therefore ready to leave and take up residence or farming elsewhere in the society.

Historian John Tobias believes that post-confederation federal Indian reserves policies were based on the policies contained in early Indian Acts:

The government expected Indians to become farmers.

In 1869, the goals of civilization and assimilation were formally added (to the prior goal of protection of Indian reserve lands) by the passage of 'an Act for the gradual enfranchisement of Indians.' The title of this piece of legislation demonstrates a change in emphasis. Whereas colonial legislation (pre-confederation) was 'for the gradual civilization,' this new act was 'for the gradual enfranchisement' of the Indian.[6]

Future Indian Acts were modified somewhat regarding enfranchisement clauses, which specified conditions under which Indian peoples would receive legal status as Canadian citizens. However, the goal of the government to assimilate, or absorb, the Indian peoples into the Canadian culture, remained constant.

The size of the reserves was another related area of misunderstanding. Many Indian leaders described huge areas of land that they believed were promised in the treaties. The commissioners never explained the actual meaning or size of a square mile.

Once the reserves were surveyed, they often did not include nearly the amount of land that the Indians had assumed to be their home base.

One chief, James Seenum of Saddle Lake, Alberta, travelled to Regina in 1884 and successfully negotiated a larger reserve directly with the Indian commissioner. The Saddle Lake Band received a reserve based on the peak population, rather than simply the population base when the surveyor arrived in the decade following Treaty Six.

Clearly, certain aspects of the treaties were implemented by the government. Dominion surveyor J. C. Nelson surveyed many Indian reserves in Alberta, Manitoba and Saskatchewan in the 1880s. Nelson used the Indian agents' head count at the time of his survey. He sometimes added a small percentage of land for good measure. As a result, many bands on the southern prairies received reserve lands to which they were entitled under treaty. However, some northern bands did not request their reserve land until years after their treaties had been signed.

There were very basic misunderstandings concerning the nature and size of the reserve land deal in the treaties. As well, the slow pace or failure to fulfill treaty promises led to a growing feeling of betrayal within the Indian communities.

Sharing Ideas

1. What importance did reserve lands have for the Indian peoples, and for the federal government?

2. There were many areas of misunderstanding regarding implementation of treaties. What were the conflicts concerning:
   a) the size of reservations,
   b) hunting, fishing and trapping rights,
   c) timber, animals and mineral ownership,
   d) the legal status of Indians, and
   e) the cost of treaty implementation?

Investigating Issues

1. "Indians should become the same as all other Canadians." From your knowledge of history and the situation in Canada today, debate the statement above.

2. Research and then compare what the Indians received through treaties with what the settlers received in homesteads in Canada. Did the Indians receive fair value for their land?

Key Words

Assimilate To absorb one group completely into the culture of another.

Enfranchise To gain full legal status as a citizen of a country or a member of a group.

Expenditure The amount of money spent from time to time.

Implement To carry out or accomplish.

What did the government impose on the Indians?

There were several government policies that were never brought up at treaty negotiations. These policies could be described as the federal government's "hidden agenda."

Indian legislation was never discussed with Indian representatives during treaty negotiations, even though the government decided that the Indian Act of 1876 would be applied to western treaty Indians.

This first Indian Act combined previous Indian legislation. The Minister of the Interior, David Laird, who served the following year as Treaty Seven Commissioner, told Parliament on March 30, 1876, that, "Indians must either be treated as minors or white men." The implementation of this Indian Act made it clear that the government

regarded itself as the guardian of these Indian minors.

The impact of this legislation often conflicted with the understandings reached at treaty negotiations. The government used the legislation to control Indian people after the treaties were signed.

This legislative control was exerted in almost all aspects of life in Indian communities. The examples which follow show how the government used this legislation to completely dominate the lives of the Indian people.

Over a period of time, a number of changes were made to the Indian Act. In politics, a municipal form of elected government was imposed. In economics, Indian products could only be sold by an Indian Agent. The agent was a government representative in charge of all matters on an Indian reserve. In culture, every effort was made to stamp out Indian customs and languages.

When it came to difficult decisions, the federal government tended to rely on the Indian Act, not on the treaties. This eroded the relationship between the Indian peoples and the government. If the federal government did not approve of Indian behaviour or actions, it could change the legislation. The government gained the legal authority to force the Indian peoples to comply with government plans.

The government acquired even more control when it created the

Under the Indian Act, Indian people required a pass to travel when leaving their reserves.

The Blackfoot meet with an Indian Agent, seated by the window, after the sale of a large portion of the reserve in 1918.

Indian Affairs Department in 1880. This department placed enormous power in the hands of the Indian agent and his superiors in Ottawa. These civil servants worked closely with the government in power.

Parliament was required to annually vote sufficient funds to implement the treaties. In turn, the public treasury depended on the taxes generated from Canadian citizens and companies. Most of these taxpayers were located in central and eastern Canada. If the federal Cabinet or senior civil servants did not recommend that sufficient monies be voted by Parliament to implement the treaties, then it simply did not happen.

These senior public officials also believed that the Indian peoples of Canada must be absorbed into their "superior" culture. This superior attitude of most 19th century Canadians towards Indians has been described as the "civilizing/ christianizing role." This attitude of the government was particularly devastating when it came to the education promises of the treaties.

At the treaty negotiations, the chiefs asked that their children have the opportunity to learn new ways of survival in a rapidly-changing environment. For the chiefs, this did not mean a loss of Indian cultural traditions. This opportunity was seen as a way to gain the benefits of a different tradition of learning from the non-Native society.

The Canadian government and the churches, however, had

something else in mind. They intended to absorb Indian children into the "civilized" Christian society of small farmers.

Indian children were not allowed to speak their language in the schools. Other aspects of Indian culture such as clothes, hairstyles and religious ceremonies were not tolerated.

Historians have concluded that the failure of Indian education in general, and residential, or live-in, schooling in particular, can be attributed to government underfunding and Indian resistance.

The residential schools were funded by the government and managed by the Catholic, Anglican, Presbyterian and Methodist churches.

"Day schools" were located near the reserves and regional "industrial schools" were located some distance away.

The industrial schools emphasized practical farming or home economics skills, along with the more standard academic program. The students were taught to be practical, thrifty and obedient. The federal government's overall goal was to force Indian people and their children to integrate into the dominant society. The children were stripped of their Indian culture, language and traditions. The health and safety conditions of these schools were often very poor, and tuberculosis was widespread.

Indian resistance involved both subtle and direct conflict with

Indian Act legislation made Indian religious traditions like the Potlatch ceremony illegal.

Children attending residential schools were stripped of their culture, language and traditions.

government authorities. Some Indian parents would not let their children go to the schools. Children often ran away from the schools after being forcefully taken from their families by Indian Agents.

The apparently simple treaty promises to provide schools and teachers on reserves proved to be a very controversial matter between Indian families, and the government and churches.

Federal authorities sought to ban Indian cultural practices in general.

Through Indian Act legislation, particularly after 1925, Indian Sun Dances, sweat lodges, potlatch ceremonies and pow wows were made illegal.

Indians resisted this express form of government coercion, or extreme pressure.

They held their dances and sacred ceremonies in secret. Indian culture went underground. It was not until 1951 that the Indian Act was changed by Parliament to make these practices legal.

UNIT 3

Sharing Ideas

1. List some of the financial reasons for inadequate fulfillment of treaty promises.

2. Describe how the federal government was able to gain legal authority over Indian people.

3. State the purpose of the federal Department of Indian Affairs. Was this purpose the same in law as in practice?

4. Why was the Indian language and other aspects of Indian culture, like dress and religion, not allowed in schools?

5. Is the term "coercion" appropriate in describing the historical experiences of Canadian Indians? Explain why it is an appropriate term, or why it is inappropriate.

Investigating Issues

1. Describe the value conflict over schooling from the Indian perspective and the government's perspective.

2. What long-term impact did the Indian Act have on Indian communities? (Note: *Where the Spirit Lives* is a documentary commenting on Indian life in residential schools.)

Key Words

Civil servant A person who works for the government.

Coercion The act of restraining or dominating by force or threat of force.

Controversial Questionable or open to disagreement.

Indian Act The principal federal statute dealing with Indian status, local government and the management of reserve lands and communal monies.

Minor A person who is under the age at which he/she is recognized by the law.

Municipal Local, county, town or city government.

Residential schools Schools created by churches where Indian students had to reside for the duration of their schooling.

How did provincial governments get involved in treaty promises?

In 1930, the Government of Canada signed Natural Resource Transfer Agreements with Manitoba, Saskatchewan and Alberta. The agreements marked the beginning of significant prairie provincial government involvement in treaty land entitlement. The Indian peoples were not included in these negotiations, and were upset that they were never consulted by the federal government.

British Columbia, Ontario, Quebec, Nova Scotia and New Brunswick had already received constitutional control, or jurisdiction, over land and natural resources. This happened under Section 109 of the British North America Act. The 1930 agreements gave equal provincial rights and status to Manitoba, Saskatchewan and Alberta.

In the negotiations leading up to the transfer agreements, D. C. Scott, Deputy Superintendent General of Indian Affairs, tried to maintain federal control over treaty land rights matters. He also tried to protect traditional Indian hunting and fishing. He was only partially successful.

From the Federal/Provincial Resource Agreements with Alberta, Saskatchewan and Manitoba

All land included in Indian reserves within the province, including those selected and surveyed but not yet confirmed, as well as those confirmed, shall continue to be vested in the Crown and administered by the Government of Canada for the purposes of Canada, and the Province will from time to time, upon the request of the Superintendent General of Indian Affairs, set aside, out of the unoccupied Crown lands hereby transferred to its administration, such further areas as the said Superintendent General may, in agreement with the appropriate Minister of the Province, select as necessary to enable Canada to fulfill its obligations under the treaties with the Indians of the Province, and such areas shall thereafter be administered by Canada in the same way in all respects as if they had never passed to the Province under the provisions hereof.

In order to secure to the Indians of the Province the continuance of the supply of game and fish for their support and subsistence, Canada agrees that the laws respecting game in force in the Province from time to time shall apply to Indians within the boundaries thereof provided, however, that the said Indians shall have the rights which the Province hereby assures to them, of hunting, fishing and trapping for game and fish for food at all seasons of the year on all unoccupied Crown lands and on any other lands to which the said Indians may have a right of access.

In negotiations, Manitoba pushed for greater provincial involvement in treaty land entitlement matters and successfully negotiated direct provincial participation.

The prairie provincial governments were also given more involvement over Indian treaty rights to hunt, fish and trap.

Over the years following 1930, there have been different interpretations of the meaning of Indian treaty rights to hunt, fish and trap, particularly in the northern regions of Alberta, Manitoba and Saskatchewan. This has led to numerous court cases when provincial wildlife officers have pressed charges against Indian hunters and fishermen. These court cases involved such matters as hunting seasons, quantities of game and access to land and water areas. The provincial governments considered these areas to be required for other purposes.

For example, in the 1970s, an Indian from Saskatchewan was charged by an Alberta wildlife officer with violating the residency provisions of Alberta's game laws. The Treaty Six Indian, Alex Frank, was hunting, and killed a moose within his own treaty area, which extends from Saskatchewan into Alberta. This case eventually involved a lengthy court battle and the Supreme Court of Canada. It decided in favour of the Indian hunting rights with Treaty Six boundaries, not provincial boundaries, being applied.

Court cases over hunting, fishing and trapping rights have caused a lot of hard feelings between the provincial governments and Indian peoples.

Different interpretations of treaty rights to hunt, fish and trap have led to numerous court cases.

Sharing Ideas

1. When and why did the federal government transfer the land and natural resources to the provincial governments of Manitoba, Saskatchewan and Alberta?

2. Describe how the federal government protected the rights to reserve land and hunting rights of treaty Indians on the prairies in these agreements.

3. Do you think that having a third party — the provincial government — involved would likely make negotiations over further reserve land selection easier or more difficult? Why or why not?

4. Did the provincial governments have the same interpretations of treaty rights to hunt, fish and trap as the Indian people? Compare and contrast the differences and similarities in the intrepretation of treaty rights.

Investigating Issues

1. Highlight some of the more recent controversies involving Indian hunting, fishing and trapping rights issues in your area. Identify the conflict and possible alternatives to resolve the conflict.

2. What role could Indian people play in conservation and environmental protection? How would this affect the interests of other parties (provincial governments, industries, tourism, etc.)?

Key Words

Jurisdiction The power, right or authority to interpret and apply the law within a given territory.

Treaty land entitlements Indian claims for reserve lands that have not yet been given under the treaties.

Vested Placed in permanent possession or control of a person or persons.

How did the Indians react to government neglect of treaties?

By 1910, an Indian protest movement began in southern Saskatchewan. This movement was led by some of the elders and older men who had negotiated Treaty Four.

In 1911, a delegation of chiefs went to Ottawa to protest to the Minister of the Interior that the Indian treaties were being broken.

The chiefs objected to the ban on Indian ceremonies and the removal from time to time of chiefs and councils by the government. They also protested against Indians not being allowed to control what was happening on reserves.

Indian resistance was becoming more organized in the 1920s and 1930s. It was fueled by neglect of treaty implementation, and legislation contrary to treaty promises.

In the 1920s, the League of Indians of Canada emerged. Several of the activists in this movement were Indian veterans returning from World War I.

The first leader of the league was Fred Loft, a Mohawk chief from Ontario. However, the most active leadership came from western Canada, particularly the Treaty Six area in Saskatchewan and Alberta.

Edward Ahanakew was the president of the league for western Canada. Large numbers of treaty Indians attended meetings of this new Indian organization. More than 1 500 attended a meeting at the Samson reserve in Alberta in 1922.

In 1932, over 1 300 members of the League met in Saddle Lake, Alberta. There, they passed a resolution requesting the government abolish the amendments to the Indian Act and closely follow Treaty Six "as made by her Majesty Queen Victoria."

The government's response was:

> Too vague. What amendments are to be abolished? They have all been carefully thought out.[7]

From the League of Indians in Western Canada, the Indian Association of Alberta was born in 1939. The Federation of Saskatchewan Indians was formed in 1944. It was these organizations that made presentations in 1946 through 1948 to the joint Senate-House of Commons committee studying changes to the Indian Act. Treaty rights continued to be a concern for these organizations. This concern continues on to the present day.

Throughout the last century, Indian resistance has been coupled with strong feelings of betrayal. Historian John Foster interprets these feelings of betrayal:

> The Indian's [complaints], revolving around such apparently [diverse] issues as hunting, trapping and fishing rights, land claims, health services, control of education, and economic development has a common denominator. A sense of betrayal underlies the words of Indian spokesmen, be they relatively young, politicized leaders or elders on the

reserves relating past experience to current circumstances. This sense of betrayal is in essence a historical interpretation. It suggests that at some point in the past, an agreement, an understanding, a pact, a contract, call it what you will, existed between the Indian and white communities. With the passage of time, through acts of omission and commission, the white community has [denied] its responsibilities. It has failed to keep the faith.[8]

Another historian, Jean Friesen, notes how government failed to keep up its side of the treaty relationships:

The west was a 'Magnificent Gift,' . . . But the acceptance of the bounty required, in the eyes of the Indians, a reciprocal balance of gifts from Canada . . . In Indian political thought the treaties represented continuing political and economic relations of mutual obligation. But in the decades after the conclusion of the treaties the burden of ensuring that these obligations be kept fell to the Indians. Their frequent requests by letter, petition . . . for fulfillment of promises filled the department's archives . . . To the Indians, disillusioned with the government's unilateral interpretations, increasingly confined in their economic opportunities, and ruled by a federal Indian Act to which they had never consented, the treaties came to be seen in the words of a Saskatchewan chief as merely 'Sweet Promises.'[9]

As Canada entered into the period following World War II, there was already a legacy of concerns and grievances regarding treaty rights implementation and interpretation.

As early as 1881, Crowfoot met with the Marquis of Lorne, Governor General of Canada, to protest government neglect of treaty promises.

73

Sharing Ideas

1. Trace the development of Indian resistance and organization from 1910 to 1948.

2. Summarize the main Indian grievances with the Canadian government since the treaties.

Investigating Issues

1. Project:

   Set up a negotiating situation between an Indian band, and the federal and provincial governments with the following facts:
   - Establishment of an Indian reserve was agreed to by all parties, and
   - The band demands $150 million social and economic package of benefits as a compensation package for loss and use of land due to industrial development. Neither government agrees to the compensation package. The federal government offers $50 million over twenty-five years for housing and economic development.

   The groups should divide up into three teams: the Indian band, and federal and provincial governments. Plan strategies for dealing with this negotiation.

Key Words

Abolish To put an end to, terminate or delete.

Activist A person that takes direct action in support of or in opposition to a controversial issue.

Archive A place in which public records or historical documents are kept and preserved.

Grievance Cause for complaint.

Section II
Contemporary Situation

The birth of Canadian Indian political organizations, starting in the 1920s, resulted in treaty rights concerns being presented to Parliament in the late 1940s.

Significant post World War II development and changes included:
- Citizen groups pressure on governments to respond to Indian needs increased from the late 1940s and beyond;
- In 1951, some of the more repressive aspects of the Indian Act, such as bans on cultural practices, were deleted. However, ultimate control of Indian peoples still remained with the Government of Canada;
- New school systems were instituted as more Indian children were educated in provincial schools. The church residential schools were dismantled by the 1960s; and
- The Civil Rights Movement in the United States in the 1960s inspired North American Indians to fight racism and prejudice as well.

Federal-provincial cooperation developed in the 1960s, as both levels of government sought to respond to the Native social needs.

These changes made an impact on Canadian society, but significant and rapid change happened after 1968. It was not, however, until the 1970s and 1980s that significant progress and some concrete resolution of outstanding treaty rights grievances can be seen.

Self-government is likely to be a major focus for continued discussion and controversy in the 1990s between Indian First Nations and the federal and provincial governments. Self-government, from a Native perspective, flows from a land base. Once a land claim has been established, the next concern tends to shift to forms of government and economic self-sufficiency. In the area of economic development there is much more consensus among Natives and governments.

Education, particularly rights to post-secondary education, is similarly very controversial when Indians assert a treaty right to education. It is linked to self-governance of Indian communities. Indian leaders assert that self-reliance must begin at home with educated and highly-skilled leaders and program administrators. In addition, education is the basis for most successful economic development enterprises, and thus represents a key priority for aboriginal peoples.

Chapter 4
Policy Changes and Land Claims

The fundamental points we had to achieve were the preservation and protection of our traditional way of life. Certain modifications to the project to minimize the negative ecological effects; suitable land; hunting, fishing and trapping rights; control of our own institutions; adequate monetary compensation; and participation in the development of the territory.

— Quebec Cree Chief Billy Diamond, 1974

What key events of the 1970s made changes in Indian policy possible?

Unresolved treaty rights issues came to public attention most dramatically in 1969. That year the new government of Prime Minister Pierre Elliot Trudeau introduced its *White Paper on Indian Policy*. It contained a number of statements relating to Indian treaty rights:

The terms and effects of the treaties between Indian people and the government have been widely misunderstood. A plain reading of the words used in the treaties reveals the limited and minimal promises that were included in them . . .
The government and the Indian people must reach a common understanding of the future role of the treaties . . . Finally, once Indian lands are firmly within Indian control, the [exception of having] treaties between groups within society and the government of that society will require that these treaties be reviewed to see how they might be equitably ended.[1]

Prime Minister Trudeau felt treaties are international agreements between nation states and that the federal government should not have treaties within Canadian society.

The government also did not believe the aboriginal rights claims in large parts of Canada. These claims included parts of Quebec, the Maritimes, the Northwest Territories, the Yukon and British Columbia.

The White Paper stated that aboriginal claims to land are too general and undefined:

> . . . it is not realistic to think of them as specific claims capable of remedy except through a policy and program that will end injustice to Indians as members of the Canadian community.[2]

The government also announced it was appointing a commission to research and investigate how treaty rights claims might be handled.

In 1969, Prime Minister Pierre Trudeau's government introduced its white paper relating to Indian treaty rights.

The White Paper brought a storm of protest by Indian bands across Canada.

Their concern went beyond treaty and aboriginal rights. The government's new policy would have wiped out the special constitutional status of "Indians and lands reserved for Indians" under the BNA Act. Indians would lose the federal government as a trustee of their rights and would receive services from provincial governments.

The *White Paper on Indian Policy* would mean a loss of special status and rights. By June of 1970, Indian chiefs of Alberta and representatives had drafted their own statement of Indian rights. This statement was titled "Citizens Plus." It was usually referred to as "The Red Paper." It represented a solid counterattack to the government's proposed policy. Manitoba Indian tribes also produced their own paper, which was titled "Wahbung, Our Tomorrows." This paper dealt in two sections with "Ongoing Relationships" (including treaties) and "Development Areas" (including economic development and reserve government).

Indian concerns are best captured by the phrase at the start of the Alberta Red Paper: "For us who are treaty Indians, there is nothing more important than our treaties, our lands and the well-being of our future generations."

The Red Paper presented a counter-argument for every major proposal put forward by the government.

Lead by National Indian Brotherhood President George Manuel and Alberta Indian leader Harold Cardinal, a delegation met with the government in 1970. With the support of many Canadian citizens, the delegation convinced the government to withdraw its white paper.

After this confrontation, the government sought a new approach.

Harold Cardinal and other Indian leaders met with Prime Minister Trudeau and his Indian Affairs Minister, Jean Chrétien in 1970 to convince the government to withdraw its white paper.

A Summary Comparison of the
Government "White Paper" and the Indians "Red Paper"

WHITE PAPER	RED PAPER
1. The legislature and constitutional bases of discrimination should be removed.	1. The legislature and constitutional bases for Indian Status and rights should be maintained until such time as Indian People are prepared and willing to renegotiate them.
2. There should be a positive recognition of the unique contribution of Indian culture on Canadian life.	2. These are nice sounding words which are intended to mislead everybody. The only way to maintain our culture is for us to remain as Indians.
3. Services should come through the same channels and from the same government agencies for all Canadians.	3. Indians have a right of access to the same services as are available to all Canadians plus those additional rights and privileges which were established by the British North America Act and by subsequent treaties and legislation.
4. Those who are furthest behind should be helped most.	4. These promises are bait to catch us in the trap of the rest of the policy. The Federal Government is trying to divide us Indian people so it can conquer us by saying that the poorer reserves will be helped most. Indian people and the organization they support should be given the resources and the responsibility to determine their own priorities and future lines of development.
5. Lawful obligations should be recognized.	5. If the Government meant what is said, we would be happy. But it is obvious that the Government has never bothered to learn what the treaties are and has a distorted picture of them. The Government shows that it is willfully ignorant of the bargains that are made. Lawful obligations, including those concerned with aboriginal rights, unfulfilled promises, and treaty provisions should be recognized.
6. Control of Indian lands should be transferred to the Indian people.	6. We agree with this intent but we find that the Government is ignorant of two basic points. The Government wrongly thinks that the Indian Reserve lands are owned by the Crown. These lands are "held" by the Crown but they are Indian lands. The second error the Government commits is making the assumption that Indians can have control of their land only if they take ownership in the way that ordinary property is owned. Control of Indian lands should be maintained by the Indian people, respecting their historical and legal rights as Indians.

WHITE PAPER	RED PAPER
7. The Government would be prepared to propose to Parliament that the Indian Act be repealed and take such legislative steps as may be necessary to enable Indians to control Indian lands and to acquire title to them.	7. We reject the proposal that The Indian Act be repealed. It is essential to review it but not before the question of the treaties is settled and there is a consensus with the Indian people respecting their historical and legal rights as Indians.
8. The Government would be prepared to make funds available for Indian economic development as an interim measure.	8. We say it is not realistic to suppose that short-term assistance with economic development as an interim measure will be adequate. The promise of substantial funds must be followed by actually making these monies available for Indian social development, with the emphasis in each case to be determined by the Indians concerned. The Government should give special consideration to the proposed Alberta Indian Development System, as a possible pattern of Federal-Provincial-Indian cooperation in community development.
9. The Government would be prepared to wind up that part of the Department of Indian Affairs and Northern Development which deals with Indian affairs. The residual responsibilities of the federal government for the programs in the field of Indian affairs would be transferred to other appropriate federal departments.	9. We believe the Department of Indian Affairs, in its present archaic and paternalistic form, should be wound up. There should be established instead a smaller federal Indian agency more closely attuned to the needs of Indian people and responsible primarily for ensuring that the Queen's promises with respect to treaties and lands are kept.
10. The Government would be prepared to appoint a Royal Commission to consult with the Indians and to study and recommend acceptable procedures for the adjudication of claims.	10. We reject the appointment of a sole Commissioner because he has been appointed without consultation and by the Government itself. He is not impartial and he has no power to do anything but a whitewash job. The Government should now, in consultation with the Indians, implement its campaign promise to establish an "independent, unbiased, unprejudiced" Commission and it should have the power to call for any witnesses or documents that it, or the Indians, wish. Its judgements would be binding.

Source: Indian Associ

In 1973, the Supreme Court in Ottawa traced aboriginal rights to the Royal Proclamation of 1763.

Indian Affairs Minister Jean Chrétien announced: "The future direction will be that which emerges in meetings between Government and Indian representatives and people."

An approach to the development of Indian policy, which emphasized consultation, was slowly emerging. Indian leaders had been able to organize their resources and public opinion in a way that forced the government to change direction.

In 1973, the Supreme Court of Canada issued its decision on the aboriginal rights claim of the Nishga Indians of British Columbia. The Supreme Court judges held that aboriginal rights do exist. Its decision stated that the Royal Proclamation of 1763, and subsequent government implementation of that proclamation, established the legal basis of aboriginal rights. As well, Indian occupation of traditional territories established the factual basis of these rights. Six of the seven judges also agreed that aboriginal title existed "dependent on the goodwill of the sovereign."

This Supreme Court decision had a definite impact on Prime Minister Trudeau's thinking and on federal Indian policy. Through its 1973 Claims Policy Statement, the federal government essentially changed direction from its 1969 White Paper. The new policy stated:

> As the government pledged some years ago, lawful obligations must be recognized. This remains the basis of government policy. The Federal government's commitment to honour the Treaties was most recently restated by Her Majesty.
> . . . You may be assured that the Government of Canada recognizes the importance of full compliance with the spirit and terms of your treaties.[3]

The addition of the word "spirit" opened the doors for discussion of the intent and meaning of the treaties.

The policy statement also made reference to aboriginal rights:

> The present statement is concerned with claims and proposals for the settlement of long-standing grievances. These claims come from groups of Indian people who have not entered into Treaty relationship with the Crown . . . In essence these claims relate to the loss of traditional use and occupancy of lands in certain parts of Canada where Indian title was never extinguished by treaty or [undone] by law . . . the lands in

question lie in British Columbia, Northern Quebec, the Yukon, and the Northwest Territories . . .
> The government has been fully aware that the claims are not only for money and land, but involve the loss of a way of life. Any settlement, therefore, must contribute positively to a lasting solution of cultural, social and economic problems that for too long have kept the Indian and Inuit people in a disadvantaged position within the larger Canadian society.[4]

At a historic meeting in Calgary, Alberta, on July 5, 1973, the chiefs of Alberta and the Indian Association of Alberta met with Queen Elizabeth. The speeches of the Queen and Harold Cardinal at that event signalled a breakthrough toward the possibility of a new understanding of the Indian treaties.

Queen Elizabeth accepts a peace pipe from Chief Samson on behalf of the Alberta Indians during a visit to Calgary in 1973.

Address by Harold Cardinal, Indian Association of Alberta, to her Majesty, Queen Elizabeth II, July 5, 1973

On the occasion of your visit to your land and ours, we take this moment to restate and recommit ourselves to the spirit and philosophy contained in the Treaties entered into by our forefathers with Your Majesty's distinguished and beloved Great Grandmother— Queen Victoria.

Our Treaties were agreements between two peoples from different civilizations to share their resources so that each could grow and successfully meet changes brought on by the passage of time.

We shared with your Majesty much land so that Her People could develop their way of life and their institutions. Our forefathers retained for us land that we too could develop our way of life.

Our people welcomed the religions brought by Her Majesty's people for they knew that the others had their ways of communicating with the Great Spirit. Since we too had and continue to have our religions, our forefathers did not share some land including the Rocky Mountains so that they too could continue to communicate with their Creator through their natural cathedrals.

Our Treaties are agreements by two peoples to share their skills, their knowledge and their tools as each was enriched by the appearance of new eras. The Treaties are agreements by two peoples living in separate realities to build for their children a better and more beautiful way of life.

To the extent that the sharing of resources in this country has accomplished this, we are happy knowing that an easier and better way of life can also be made possible for our brothers in different parts of the globe.

Therefore, in this spirit, we are proud and happy to welcome Your Gracious Majesty to this land.

We believe it to be a historic occasion that we who have a special status under the Treaties should meet formally, for the first time with the Sovereign Queen who is our Treaty partner.

Since the Treaties were signed, the span of almost a century has brought many changes to this land. Changes that are called progress. These changes, however, have seldom meant progress for Indian people.

Ecological change, since the signing of Treaty, has destroyed to a large degree the abundance of wildlife which once provided the livelihood of our people. The resulting poverty has produced many problems which are crying for a solution.

In recent years, the Indian people of Alberta have been preparing themselves for solving these problems with the aid of Your Majesty's Government. We realize that even though we have begun our sojourn into the modern world, we have much to overcome and far to go.

We believe that a fundamental step towards solving the problems of the Indian people is for both parties to the Treaties to reaffirm their intention to uphold and respect the terms of the Treaties signed in good faith so many years ago.

We therefore welcome this opportunity to make the solemn declaration that the Indian people will continue to uphold the promises we made in the Treaties, and to reaffirm our loyalty to Your Majesty Queen Elizabeth II and to your heirs and successors.

We confidently pray that Your Majesty's Government of Canada do likewise.

We are proud to be Indians. We are also proud of the record of our people in upholding and fulfilling the Treaty promises.

We are equally proud to be Canadians and loyal and dutiful subjects of Your Majesty.

We thank you for your visit to Canada and Alberta and for the audience which you have granted us today.

Reply given by Her Majesty, Queen Elizabeth II, to address by Harold Cardinal, President of the Indian Association of Alberta, July 5, 1973.

It gives me great pleasure to meet you and the Chiefs who have come here today as representatives of the Indian people of Alberta. I thank you most warmly for your welcome and for your wise words.

The whole world has lived through sweeping changes since the days, almost 100 years ago, when your predecessors signed treaties with the representatives of the government of my great-grandmother, Queen Victoria.

Here in the West of Canada, the changes have been specially marked. Thousands of settlers came to this land in search of a new life, yet in spite of the disruption this brought to their ways, the Indian people gave them much needed help.

Now the land is transformed and life has completely changed. Large cities, intensive cultivation and all the products of this technological age have appeared as part of the new civilization which has been developed here.

It is unfortunately true that during this rapid transformation and in spite of the wealth which has been created, many Indian people have been left to live in poverty and distress. This and many other problems arising from these changes still need to be solved.

You may be confident of the continued cooperation of my government which represents your people as it represents all the people of Canada. You may be assured that my government recognizes the importance of full compliance with the spirit and terms of your treaties.

I am deeply impressed by the pride of heritage which has sustained you through so many dramatic changes and difficulties. I hope this very sense of identity will help you find you own a true Indian place in the modern world.

You have said that you are proud to be both Indians and Canadians. I am sure that your fellow Canadians are learning to appreciate and to respect the very special qualities and culture of the Indian peoples and their deep feeling for the natural environment of their homeland.

Your concern for wildlife is shared by an increasing number of interested citizens across the country.

Let us look to the future. The Indian people of Canada are entering a new phase in their relationship with other Canadians. It is my hope that in the coming years you will together find a means to combine a way of life, which suits your culture, and social aspirations, with full participation in the creation and enjoyment of the growing material wealth of Canada today.

Such an achievement will give you the opportunity to continue and to intensify your special contributions to the fabric of Canadian life.

Sharing Ideas

1. The Red Paper states "For us who are Treaty Indians, there is nothing more important than our treaties, our lands and the well-being of our future generations." Outline the reasons why the treaties are so important to the Indian peoples of Canada.

2. Detail the significance of the Supreme Court decision of the Nishga Indians in British Columbia.

3. The federal government realized that a consultation process with Indians was necessary to resolve outstanding concerns. Identify the factors that brought about this "change of heart."

4. Harold Cardinal reviews the many aspects of sharing the land, religion, technology, skills and resources, but claims that time and change has not meant progress for the Indians. Assess the negative effects change has had for the Indian people. Suggest some actions that could be taken to diminish these negative aspects of change.

5. Explain why the meeting with Queen Elizabeth was so important for the Indian peoples.

Investigating Issues

1. Compare and contrast the 1969 and 1973 federal policies on treaty and aboriginal rights to land. What prompted the change?

2. Look at the charts of the White Paper and the reaction in the Red Paper. Identify the major obstacles to negotiating land claims, the different views concerning treaty rights, and the future of the Indian Act and the Department of Indian Affairs.

Key Words

Aboriginal Original, indigenous or first peoples of an area. The earliest inhabitants of a country.

Aboriginal rights Special rights held by aboriginal people, such as the right to fish and hunt game.

Confrontation Challenging or meeting in a hostile manner.

Consultation The act of asking advice of or seeking council from another.

Trustee One appointed to manage the affairs of another.

Did the James Bay and Northern Quebec Agreement of 1975 indicate a change in policy?

In 1971, Quebec Premier Robert Bourassa announced plans for a major hydro-electric development in the James Bay area in northern Quebec. There had been, however, no consultation with the eight Cree communities in the area. Nor had there been any consideration of the social, political and economic impact on these people.

Young Cree leaders met with people from each village in the area. A decision was made to oppose, or at least demand changes to, the hydro-electric project. The Cree people feared the proposed project would harm the fish and wildlife habitat. This would destroy the livelihood of this traditional hunting society.

The Cree began negotiations with the Quebec government. Under the 1912 Quebec Boundaries Extension Act, the government had a legal obligation to negotiate treaties with the Indian tribes in the area.

The Cree also tried to enlist the support of the federal government. However, the federal government chose to remain neutral. By the fall of 1972, it became clear to the Cree of James Bay that serious negotiations with the Quebec and Canadian governments was not possible.

The James Bay Cree launched a legal action in the provincial court of Quebec. This action declared their traditional occupancy and continued use of the area for hunting, fishing and trapping. They were asserting their Indian title to the land and asking the court to recognize this right. In particular, the Cree requested the court grant a temporary restraining order to stop the project until their land rights were recognized and a treaty was negotiated with them. In this way, the rights of the Cree could be protected before the development had proceeded too far. By this time, construction on the project had begun. Construction camps and roads were already in place.

From the 1912 Quebec Boundaries Extension Act

. . . That the province of Quebec will recognize the rights of the Indian inhabitants in the territory above described to the same extent, and will obtain surrenders of such rights in the same manner, as the Government of Canada has heretofore recognized such rights and has obtained surrender thereof, and the said province shall bear and satisfy all charges and expenditures in connection with or arising out of such surrenders;

That no such surrender shall be made or obtained except with the approval of the Governor in Council;

That the trusteeship of the Indians in the said territory, and the management of any lands now or hereafter reserved for their use, shall remain in the Government of Canada subject to the control of Parliament.

Government of Quebec lawyers opposed the Cree request. They argued that the Cree did not have aboriginal title and that the project was not harming the land as stated by the Cree.

In November of 1973, extensive evidence was presented by expert witnesses at a long court hearing. The court ruled that the Cree Indian and the Inuit people:

In 1971, the Quebec government announced that construction would begin on a hydro-electric dam in the traditional hunting and trapping areas of the Cree in the James Bay area.

. . . have been in possession and occupation of these lands and exercising fishing, hunting, and trapping rights therein since time immemorial. It has been shown that the Government of Canada entered into treaties wherever it desired to obtain land for the purposes of settlement or otherwise. In view of the obligation assumed by the Province of Quebec in the legislation of 1912, it appears that the Province of Quebec cannot develop or otherwise open up these lands for settlement without acting in the same manner, that is, without prior agreement of the Indians and [Inuit].[5]

In other words, the judge ruled that the hydro-electric development should not have proceeded before a treaty was negotiated between Quebec, Canada, and the Indians and Inuit of northern Quebec.

This court judgement represented a clear court victory for the James Bay Cree. It is generally agreed that this court action was instrumental in changing the attitude and policy of the Quebec government.

Quebec now saw the necessity of negotiations with the James Bay Cree and their Inuit neighbours. The Canadian government also recognized the need to negotiate, as required under the 1973 claims policy for aboriginal rights.

The resulting Quebec/Cree/Inuit/Canada negotiations began in 1974. There were a wide range of topics. Each party to the agreement brought a team of experts to assist them.

Quebec Cree Chief Billy Diamond outlined the minimum demands that the Cree people of

James Bay believed were necessary for their survival:

> The fundamental points we had to achieve were the preservation and protection of our traditional way of life; certain modifications to the project to minimize the negative ecological effects; suitable land, hunting, fishing and trapping rights; control of our own institutions; adequate monetary compensation; and participation in the development of the territory.[6]

On November 11, 1975 the 450-page James Bay and Northern Quebec Agreement was signed between the James Bay Cree and the Quebec Inuit, the Quebec and Canadian governments, and the hydro-electric companies.

Chief Diamond, in a speech a decade later, described the benefits of the agreement, which involved land surrender of approximately 410 000 square miles (1 061 900 sq. km):

> The agreement recognizes exclusive native hunting, fishing and trapping rights over virtually all of our traditional territory . . . the agreement also establishes a system of Cree and Inuit local government and a Cree school board, giving us substantial control over the education of our children; it establishes a Cree regional board of health and social services; it provides for Cree police forces and extensive control over the administration of justice; it provides for serious economic and social development resources and for monetary compensation for the Crees from the governments of Quebec and Canada as well as special corporations to manage the compensation.[7]

The benefits included traditional rights, as well as new rights to control over health, education and justice in their communities. Social and economic development would also be addressed through the financial compensation portions of the agreement. The Cree have made remarkable strides forward in terms of controlling and shaping their own future.

With the advantage of hindsight in the last half of the 1980s, the James Bay Cree and many observers

The governments of Quebec and Canada negotiated an agreement with the Cree and Inuit people of northern Quebec.

believe there are fewer problems with the agreement itself than with the implementation of the agreement. This is similar to the problems with treaty implementation in the west.

One problem involves both levels of government being willing to follow through on certain financial aspects in the agreement. Another problem is related to unforeseen environmental impacts.

Four key areas of the agreement have been assessed this way:

1. The agreement has considerably aided Cree hunting;
2. It has strengthened the Cree economically, socially and politically;
3. Government respect and support for the agreement have been mixed and uneven; and
4. The Cree are more autonomous now than before the agreement but threats to Cree autonomy remain.[8]

There was some concrete evidence of the changes for the Cree in the decade following the agreement:

1. There was an increase in the number of Cree hunters from 700 to 1 100 (about 50 percent of the work force);
2. Cree businesses had been developed (for example, a joint venture with a Japanese firm for a special boat and Cree ownership of an airline); and
3. A tenfold increase in the number of people employed in administration, social work education, and health services.

Another hydro-electric project, James Bay II, has been announced, and the Cree have already stated their opposition to the new development, primarily on environmental grounds.

The James Bay Agreement led the way for other modern-day treaties.

In 1984, the Inuvialuit of the western arctic signed the second treaty of the modern era with the federal government. This treaty also involved certain land rights, including surface and subsurface ownership of land and natural resources, surface ownership to other lands, and hunting, fishing and trapping rights to a much larger area. The Inuvialuit final agreement also included $152 million in compensation and other benefits.

By the end of the 1980s, the federal government had signed agreements-in-principle with the remaining Native organizations in northern Canada. These included the Dene-Metis of the Northwest Territories, The Council of Yukon Indians and the Tungavik Federation of Nunavut (eastern Arctic).

Even if these agreements-in-principle resulted in final settlements, many claims would remain. No agreements exist in British Columbia or the Maritimes. Indian peoples in these areas still have no treaties. Modern treaties are sure to continue for some time to come.

Indian-governmental relations are constantly changing in Canada. For example, British Columbia

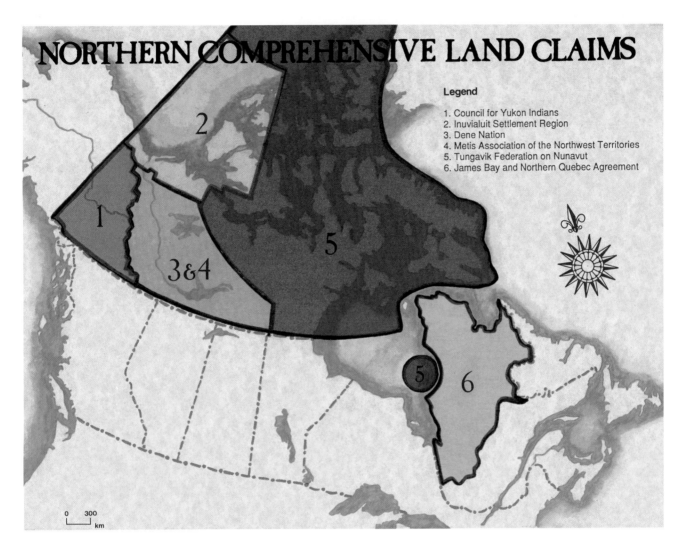

NORTHERN COMPREHENSIVE LAND CLAIMS

Legend

1. Council for Yukon Indians
2. Inuvialuit Settlement Region
3. Dene Nation
4. Metis Association of the Northwest Territories
5. Tungavik Federation on Nunavut
6. James Bay and Northern Quebec Agreement

0   300
km

announced in the summer of 1990 that it was prepared to negotiate aboriginal claims.

In the fall of 1990, negotiations began between British Columbia, Canada and the Nishga Indian peoples of northern British Columbia to settle that outstanding aboriginal rights claim. On the other hand, the Dene and Metis of the Northwest Territories have rejected their agreement-in-principle with Canada. The future will no doubt bring more changes.

Sharing Ideas

1. Describe the initial concern the Cree in northern Quebec had to the proposed hydro-electric development.

2. Did the Cree have a legal right to be consulted?

3. Briefly sum up the implications which lead up to, and resulted from, this hydro-electric project. What future implications did this ruling have for:
   a) the Indian people in other provinces, and
   b) the government of Canada?

4. Summarize and outline the specific terms of the James Bay Agreement which gave the Indians control of many aspects of their lives.

Investigating Issues

1. Do you think the assurances and compensation to the Cree were adequate or inadequate? Was the resolution an effective compromise?

2. Research the current status of comprehensive land claims based on aboriginal rights claims in Canada (for example, British Columbia and the Northwest Territories), noting the concerns of Native groups, the geographic area, and the present status of negotiations.

3. What relationship is there between areas which are subject to comprehensive land claims and areas covered by treaties?

Key Words

Autonomous Self-governing.

Habitat The place where a plant or animal naturally lives or grows.

Why are there still outstanding land claims in areas which have treaties?

There continues to be a growing number of Indian land claims in Canada. Not all land claims occur in areas which have no treaties. In fact, the treaties themselves are at the root of most land claims.

After the treaties were signed, the government did not fulfill all of its commitments. In some instances, the government did not follow through on treaty promises, or it disposed of reserve lands and assets without proper permission.

Indian people feel that the federal government has a trust responsibility for the Indian lands and assets. They feel that some of the actions taken by the government over the years have violated this responsibility.

Consequently, many claims have been made against their trustee.

Claims which are based on aboriginal rights, and traditional use and occupancy of the land are called comprehensive claims. For example, the James Bay Agreement resulted from a comprehensive claim.

Claims which are based on treaties and the administration of Indian lands, assets and fulfillment of treaties are called specific claims.

In general, specific claims can be divided into three types:

1. Treaty land entitlement claims relate to Indian requests for reserve lands that have not been fulfilled under treaties;

Years of inaction on specific claims have contributed to Indian frustration and unrest.

2. Land surrender claims involve legally improper surrenders of Indian reserve lands; and

3. Indian asset claims refer to Indian monies or resources, which were held in trust for Indian bands by the government, but were not properly managed.

The federal government's 1973 claims policy stated: "You must be assured that the Government of Canada recognizes the importance of full compliance with the spirit and terms of your treaties." This policy was meant to show Canada's willingness to fulfill lawful obligations when implementing the treaties.

In each specific claim, an Indian band must submit its researched claim to the Departments of Indian Affairs and Justice of the federal government. After a historical and legal review of the claim, the government decides if it agrees with the claim. If the government agrees, it views the Indian claim as properly falling under its lawful obligation policy. It then negotiates with the Indian band to try to settle the claim. Sometimes, land surrender and Indian asset claims are settled between the federal government and the respective Indian bands. Negotiations for land entitlement claims involve the federal and provincial governments, and the Indian band.

A 1990 federal government report gives an overview of the specific claims situation:

> . . . 578 specific claims have been submitted . . ., of which 205 have been resolved and a further 275 are currently at various stages of review. Since 1984, 23 specific claims have been settled with more than $75 million paid in compensation and nearly [40 000 hectares] of land provided to Indian bands.[9]

Examples of settled specific claims include:

- Saskatchewan — February, 1986: $19 million claim settlement with the White Bear Indian Reserve;
- Alberta — December, 1986: $26.6 million and 5 000 hectare land entitlement settlement reached with the Fort Chipewyan Cree Band;
- British Columbia — July, 1989: Lower Kootenay Indian Band specific claim settled. The settlement provides the band with payments of $4.4 million.

STATUS OF SPECIFIC CLAIMS

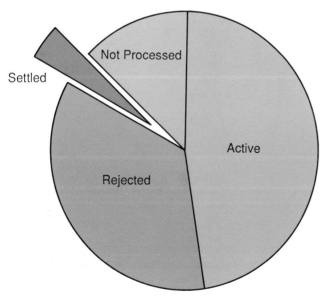

SOURCE: Statistics Division and Educational Branch, DIAND (1990)

- Ontario — July, 1986: Compensation of $7 million was paid to the Grassy Narrows and Islington communities for mercury pollution of their water resources; and
- Nova Scotia — July, 1985: A settlement of $1.2 million was paid to the Wagmacook Band as compensation for land improperly removed from the reserve. Funds were to be used to purchase replacement land on the open market.

In order to understand the history of a treaty land entitlement claim, it might be useful to review the history of one band's struggle to acquire reserve land promised in a treaty.

The Fort Chipewyan Cree band of northeastern Alberta first requested reserve land in 1922. It was not until 1986 that its treaty land entitlement claim was settled.

Treaty Eight contained the following provision for band reserve land entitlement ". . . reserves for such bands as desire reserves, the same not to exceed one square mile for each family of five for such families as may elect to reside on reserves . . ."

At the time of Treaty Eight negotiations in 1899, most northern Indian bands refused to be placed on reserves like prairie Indians. They wished to remain free to travel over a wide territory to hunt, fish and trap.

Later, some bands had to press their land claims for reserve lands because of resource developments on their traditional territories.

The Cree band at Fort Chipewyan asked for a reserve in its traditional hunting and fishing territory. This territory requested was the Lake Claire area west of Fort Chipewyan and Lake Athabasca. There were two developments in the area that threatened their treaty right to hunt, fish and trap. The federal government had established Wood Buffalo National Park west of Fort Chipewyan in the early 1920s. Further, the federal government decided that the national park boundaries should be extended south of the Peace River to protect the wintering grounds of the Wood Bison. Aggressive non-Native trappers had invaded traditional trapping areas and disregarded Indian rights.

Despite efforts over the following decades, the reserve entitlement requests of the Fort

Damage to the environment of traditional Indian lands has led to many specific claims.

95

Chipewyan Cree remained outstanding into the 1970s. Then, the Cree band began actively pursuing their reserve land entitlements again. Chief Lawrence Courtorielle took on a leadership role to press the land claim.

Several Indian bands in northern Alberta were facing powerful forces of development in the mid-1970s in northern Alberta. Oil companies were eager to extract and process oil, gas, and oil sands resources. Their efforts were aided by the governments of Alberta and Canada.

Both governments were seeking a share of the oil profits. This was seen as a major source of government revenue following the OPEC oil embargo in the mid-1970s.

Both governments tended to ignore the fact that these developments were on the traditional lands of Treaty Eight Indian bands.

The Cree Band was also instrumental in changing Alberta's policy on mineral rights. It sought a middle ground with the policy

After the treaties were signed, many new developments were undertaken in traditional hunting, fishing and trapping areas.

position of both Alberta and Canada, leaving the mineral rights matter as the one key issue of fundamental disagreement.

The Cree Band continued to negotiate all the components of the treaty land entitlement agreement. By 1986, the Fort Chipewyan Cree were able to complete a treaty land entitlement settlement essentially based on current day population figures. The entitlement included provincial and federal land, as well as money.

The Alberta policy was changed through direct negotiations and by a changing relationship with the Cree Band at Fort Chipewyan and other Indian bands.

Indian communities must make a whole range of difficult choices when it comes to land claims negotiations and settlements. They must decide:

1. which strategy to use and when;
2. what mix of land, compensation and traditional harvesting rights to settle for;
3. how to best serve the interests of the communities and the governments in order to find an appropriate mix or blend of interests for all parties; and
4. which advisors and lawyers to choose.

There is tremendous pressure on Indian leaders and communities. Many band members accuse their elected leadership of "selling out" for too few lasting benefits. The negotiation process, however, can provide real lasting land and resource benefits for the communities. The final settlement choices are extremely difficult, especially when determining the needs of future generations.

The government negotiators also have a variety of interests to satisfy. The government must consider the concerns of:

1. the general public, which elects the politicians in power;
2. the plans of business developers, such as oil and forestry companies; and
3. other citizens living near Indian communities.

In the end, negotiated settlements happen when there is a political will to settle the claims by all parties.

One of the key elements of the negotiated agreement for Indian communities at Fort Chipewyan was the evolution of a relationship of mutual respect between all parties in the negotiations. The difficult phase of implementation will determine whether this relationship can be effectively maintained.

Sharing Ideas

1. Define "specific land claim." What are the three types of specific claims? How are they different?

2. Explain why reserve land entitlements were not established for many northern bands.

3. Describe how and why the demands of the Fort Chipewyan Cree were finally resolved.

4. Analyse the importance of "relationships of mutual respect" to land claims negotiations.

Investigating Issues

1. Research a specific land claim in your area. Address the following categories:
   - a) the historic basis for the claim,
   - b) the demands of the Indian people,
   - c) the government response or position, and
   - d) the anticipated way in which you think the claim could be resolved fairly.

Key Words

Indian assets claims To assert that Indian monies or resources held in trust by the government were not properly managed or improperly disposed of.

Land surrender claims To assert that surrenders of Indian reserve lands were illegal or improper.

Chapter 5
Current Controversies

The Committee recommends that the right of Indian people to self-government be explicitly stated and entrenched in the Constitution of Canada. The surest way to achieve permanent and fundamental change in the relationship between Indian peoples and the federal government is by way of constitutional amendment. Indian first nation governments would form a distinct order of government with their jurisdiction defined.

– Report of the Special Committee on Indian Self-Government, 1983

How did the Constitution Act of 1982 affect aboriginal and treaty rights?

In the late 1970s, Prime Minister Pierre Elliot Trudeau began steps toward patriation, or bringing the Constitution back to Canada from Britain.

A federal white paper on constitutional reform titled *A Time for Action* was issued in 1978. This constitutional proposal contained a recognition of aboriginal rights and the treaty-making process. The proposal, however, did not include plans to involve aboriginal organizations in constitutional discussions. These organizations wanted aboriginal and treaty rights included in the new constitution.

To accomplish this, they would have to be heard at the constitutional talks. This proved to be difficult.

Constitutional discussions were held between provincial premiers and the prime minister. These eleven first ministers considered their own

Aboriginal leaders finally won the right to participate in constitutional meetings with the prime minister and the premiers.

Queen Elizabeth signed the Constitution Act, which recognizes aboriginal rights.

business to be of primary importance at the discussions.

Joe Clark defeated Trudeau in the 1979 election. That summer, Prime Minister Clark met with aboriginal leaders. One important result marked their meeting. "Native Peoples in the Constitution of Canada" was included as an agenda item for future first ministers' conferences on the constitution.

In 1980, Trudeau was re-elected as prime minister. The patriation issue dominated federal provincial politics for the next two years. There were conferences, court challenges and furious lobbying. It was difficult for Trudeau to find an amending formula that was acceptable to all provincial governments, as well as the Canadian Parliament.

Eventually, the federal government proposed new constitutional clauses to make the constitutional package more acceptable to more Canadian groups. Changes were made for stronger recognition of women's and Native's rights.

After negotiations with the provinces, agreement was made on the wording for Section 35 of the new constitution. The clause was of fundamental importance to the future of aboriginal peoples in Canada:

Key sections (25, 35, and 35.1) of the Constitution Act of 1982 Including the 1983 amendments

25. The guarantee in this Charter of certain rights and freedoms shall not be construed so as to abrogate or derogate from any aboriginal, treaty or other rights or freedoms that pertain to the aboriginal peoples of Canada including:

    (a) any rights or freedoms that have been recognized by the Royal Proclamation of October 7, 1763; and

    (b) any rights or freedoms that now exist by way of land claims agreements or may be so acquired.

35. (1) The existing aboriginal and treaty rights of the aboriginal peoples of Canada are hereby recognized and affirmed.

    (2) In this Act, "aboriginal peoples of Canada" includes the Indian, Inuit and Metis peoples of Canada.

    (3) For greater certainty, in Subsection (1) "treaty rights" includes rights that now exist by way of land claims agreements or may be so acquired.

    (4) Notwithstanding any other provision of this Act, the aboriginal and treaty rights referred to in Subsection (1) are guaranteed equally to male and female persons.

35.1. The Government of Canada and the provincial governments are committed to the principle that, before any amendment is made to Class 24 of Section 91 of the Constitution Act, 1987, to Section 25 of this Act or to this Part.

    (a) a constitutional conference that includes in its agenda an item relating to the proposed amendment, composed of the Prime Ministers of the provinces, will be convened by the Prime Minister of Canada; and

    (b) the Prime Minister of Canada will invite representatives of the aboriginal peoples of Canada to participate in the discussions on that item.

The existing aboriginal and treaty rights of the aboriginal peoples of Canada are hereby recognized and affirmed. . . "aboriginal peoples of Canada" includes the Indian, Inuit and Metis people of Canada.[1]

The constitutional document was signed by the Queen in Canada on April 17, 1982. It also included two additional sections dealing with the aboriginal peoples.

Section 25 provides guarantees and protection of aboriginal and treaty rights in relation to the Charter of Rights and confirms the Royal Proclamation of 1763.

Section 37 dealt with a future constitutional conference, which would include aboriginal representatives.

Section 37 was then succeeded by Section 35.1.

A series of constitutional conferences on aboriginal rights were held between 1983 and 1987.

There were key areas of agreement. For the first time the new procedure for changing the constitution was implemented. This amending formula required approval by the federal government and at least seven provinces containing no less than 50 percent of the population.

Little progress was made, however, in defining treaty and aboriginal rights. The provincial and federal governments were reluctant to accept the nature and powers of Indian self-government.

Statements by aboriginal leaders on aboriginal self-government at the First Ministers' Conferences asserted control (or jurisdiction) over Indian traditional land and resources.

Despite the failure to achieve much progress on the definition of aboriginal self-government, substantial changes were made to the Canadian Constitution. The changes may represent a turning point in the history of Canadian Indian policy.

Canadian aboriginal peoples now have a unique constitutional status among indigenous peoples of the world. In addition, women's rights were stated clearly, as both men and women were equally guaranteed rights in Section 35 (4).

It will be up to future leaders, citizens and courts to come up with a precise definition of treaty and aboriginal rights.

Many Indian women and men had been putting pressure on the federal government since the early 1970s to have the discriminatory sections of the Indian Act deleted. The Indian Act (prior to 1985) favoured men over women because women would lose their Indian status by marrying a Metis or non-Native person, whereas men, who took the same course of action did not lose their status.

Flowing from the Constitutional Act 1982, provisions for equality of men and women (Section 35.4), and the Charter of Rights and Freedoms (Section 15), changes were made to the Indian Act in 1985 by the Parliament of Canada.

This new Act titled "An Act to Amend the Indian Act" had three main goals:

Elijah Harper, a Native member of the legislature of Manitoba, helped stop the Meech Lake constitutional accord and became a symbol of aboriginal power.

1) The repeal of sexually discriminatory provisions relating to entitlement to status as an Indian under the Act;

2) The restoration of rights lost through sexual discrimination; and

3) Where requested, band control of band membership (while retaining federal control over entitlement to Indian status).[2]

This new change to the Indian Act (1985) provided that Indian men and Indian women would be treated equally in every respect. Women and the first generation of children who had lost their status under the Indian Act, could apply to become status Indians.

The new legislation, commonly known as Bill C-31, resulted in almost 40 000 people having their Indian status returned to them by 1988. These individuals had to make application and provide documentation, such as birth certificates, regarding their family background.

Many Indian bands and leaders were concerned about this provision for practical purposes. They were already experiencing shortages of housing and other services.

Some Indian bands also used the new legislation to develop their own membership codes and residency requirements, in order to more effectively regulate these developments. This is the aspect of self-government which was the third objective of the legislation.

In 1987, the constitutional focus of the federal government shifted to finding a constitutional agreement suitable to Quebec. The resulting federal-provincial agreement in principle was called the Meech Lake Accord. The recognition of Quebec as a distinct society was a major provision of the accord.

The accord also provided protection for aboriginal and treaty rights gains in the constitution. However, it left the matter of Indian self-government as an agenda item that may or may not be brought forward.

The Meech Lake process for constitutional change was brought to a halt, in part, through the actions of Elijah Harper. The Manitoba MLA said that Indian Nations are also distinct societies, and have as much right as Quebec to be considered as such.

Harper also protested the exclusion of aboriginal and other peoples from the Meech Lake decision-making process of the prime minister and the premiers.

All of this underlines the need for better communication and understanding of Native concerns by all Canadians on this and other issues affecting Canada's future as a nation.

In part, we must try to understand the collective rights, not just the individual rights of citizens in relation to governments, guaranteed in the Charter of Rights and Freedoms. Both Quebec and Native peoples consider themselves distinct societies and that these distinct societies (or nations) consider that they have rights to self-determination and other cultural rights.

These items will be on the agenda for the 1990s and beyond.

Sharing Ideas

1. Identify which changes to the Constitution in 1982 and 1983 were related to treaty and aboriginal rights.

2. Suggest reasons why aboriginal self-government turned out to be a difficult matter to negotiate.

3. Describe the goals of the new Indian Act in terms of women's rights.

Investigating Issues

1. Project: Simulation of a First Ministers' Conference
   View the National Film Board's film *Dancing Around the Table* (two parts— 50 minutes each) and form three different teams (one team representing the federal government, one the provincial government and one the aboriginal representatives). Then prepare for, and hold, your own First Ministers Conference on Aboriginal and Treaty Rights. Support and defend your view on the following: land, self-government, education, and hunting and fishing rights.

2. Compare and contrast the similarities and differences between the positions of Quebec and Indian people on the Constitution.

Key Words

Agenda The items of business to be dealt with at a meeting.

Amending formula The procedure that must be followed to make any changes to a constitution.

Constitution The core system of rules and principles by which a nation or group is governed.

First Ministers' Conference A meeting of the prime minister and provincial premiers.

Indigenous Living or occurring naturally in a region.

Meech Lake Accord The 1988 agreement made by the federal government and the provinces regarding amendments to the Canadian Constitution. The document was signed in Meech Lake, Quebec.

Patriation To bring under the direct control of the country from which it was derived or intended.

Is Indian self-government a treaty right?

Indian Bands and organizations have been pressuring governments for the right to self-determination since the 1900s.

They wanted a community-based democratic process, rather than federal control from Ottawa. The bands wanted freedom from the Indian Act and the Department of Indian Affairs.

This quest for self-determination had certain parallels to Quebec's desire in the 1960s to be "masters in our own homes" and to the independence struggles of peoples in Latin America, Asia and Africa.

Canadian Indians are a small minority of the total population in Canada. They represent about 1.5 percent of the total population. When the total number of Indian, Inuit and Metis peoples in Canada are included, the total represents about 3 percent of the population. In northern Canada, the Indian percentage of the population is much higher, especially in the Northwest Territories and the

Indian people want control over the decision-making processes which affect their communities.

Yukon. In northern parts of the prairie provinces, there are also higher native proportions of the population.

Indian bands want greater control and participation in decisions which affect their communities. All aspects of self-government would be undertaken *within* Indian reserve boundaries. Indian communities want control over a mixture of services, such as education, health care and social services. For most other Canadians, these services are provided by local, provincial or federal governments. The communities also want a leading role in developing new jobs through business enterprises.

There is a great diversity of hopes and dreams among the more than five hundred Indian bands in Canada regarding Indian self-government.

In the 1970s, the term for self-determination most often used by Indian leaders was "Indian control." By the early 1980s, this demand came to be known as "Indian self-government."

To understand some of the issues of Indian self-government, it is always useful to review and try to define terminology, such as "nations" and "first nations." Nations have been defined as:

> . . . a group of people with a common language, culture and history who identify with each other as belonging to a common political entity.[3]

It follows that "first nations" in Canada are the Indian peoples and their descendants. In other words,

the nations of peoples who were here first. Language heritage is a key aspect of the definition of nations.

In the 1980s, the use of the term "Indian first nations" replaced the term Indian bands. Indian bands, for many Indians, was simply a legal term used in the Indian Act. It did not capture the Indian way of expressing who they are. Indian first nations has now become increasingly common. The 1983 Report of the Special Committee on Indian Self-Government in Canada, also called the Penner Report, used this term.

The national organization of Indian peoples refers to itself as the Assembly of First Nations (AFN). On the prairies, the dominant Indian organization, including representatives from Saskatchewan, Alberta and Manitoba, is the Prairie Treaty Nations Alliance (PTNA).

The prairie Indians saw their interests as different from those of the national organization. They broke away from the AFN prior to the First Ministers' Conference on Treaty and Aboriginal Rights and the Constitution in 1987.

The different names of these organizations, as well as the fact of their separateness, is important. It signals another factor in this matter of self-government, namely different political perspectives within Indian communities and organizations.

Prairie Indians in the PTNA emphasize nation-to-nation relationships. The majority of AFN members talk about self-government as an aboriginal right intimately linked to their aboriginal title to land. Many of these groups are in the process of negotiating to get settlements of claims. Indian peoples who have never signed treaties believe they still have aboriginal title to the land.

Indian positions on Indian self-government contain certain differences. This is especially true of Indian First Nations that have existing treaties (Treaty Indians on the prairies and Ontario) and those who are negotiating modern treaties (Indians from British Columbia, the Yukon and the Northwest Territories).

Indian First Nations take the position that their "nationhood" was legally recognized in the Royal Proclamation of 1763. The proclamation referred to "the several nations or tribes with whom we are connected and live under our protection." This recognition was affirmed when "Chiefs and Headmen" were called upon by the Canadian government to negotiate and eventually sign the Indian treaties.

The Prairie Treaty Nation Alliance asserts that: "Nations Make Treaties — Treaties do not make Nations." They interpret the Indian treaties today as nation-to-nation, or government-to-government, agreements.

The treaties do not represent a surrender of their original right to govern themselves. Indian organizations which emphasize aboriginal rights, also use this inherent, or fundamental, rights argument. They maintain that aboriginal rights to self-government have always existed.

Most governments at both the provincial and federal levels, consider that inherent rights to Indian self-governance are not well-defined. The governments prefer to delegate, or pass on, rights. This would be done in the form of legislation in specific areas of responsibility.

Governments often view the treaties as the basis of a relationship where Indians became subjects of

A variety of Indian groups represent the different political perspectives of Indian people today.

Indian groups are worried that they will not have enough money to provide services.

the Queen. As subjects, Indian bands and individuals would conform to the British Parliamentary system of government and democracy as it has evolved in Canada.

New powers granted to Indian nations would have to be delegated by the Queen's representative in Canada, namely the federal government, which has the constitutional responsibility for Indians. How these new or renewed structures of Indian government would be financed is also a concern to everyone.

It is clear that new developmental dollars would be required to finance and establish Indian-run institutions.

The provinces do not want the federal government to place its legal and financial responsibilities for Indians on them. The Indians agree with the provinces on that matter.

As well, Indian communities do not want to take over services formerly provided by the federal government without the funds required to run the programs. The communities are concerned that they be shielded from subsequent funding cutbacks by the federal government.

Meanwhile, the ever-increasing size of the federal deficit has slowed the federal capacity to respond to these Indian hopes and dreams.

In 1983, the federal government sought a way to respond to these complex issues. They asked a Parliamentary committee to investigate the situation and bring forward recommendations concerning Indian self-government. This parliamentary committee included representatives from the Liberals, New Democrats, and Progressive Conservatives, as well as a non-voting representative of the Assembly of First Nations. It was chaired by a Liberal member, Keith Penner.

The so-called Penner Report contained a number of positive recommendations on the matter of Indian self-government. These recommendations were generally well-received. However, on certain tough issues, such as differences between inherent and delegated rights, the committee sought a compromise and used the phrase a "distinct order of government with their jurisdiction defined."

The Penner committee's first three recommendations were:

1. The Committee recommends that the federal government establish a new relationship with Indian First Nations and that an essential element of this relationship be recognition of Indian self-government;
2. The Committee recommends that the right of Indian people

to self-government be explicitly stated and entrenched in the Constitution of Canada. The surest way to achieve permanent and fundamental change in the relationship between Indian peoples and the federal government is by way of constitutional amendment. Indian First Nation governments would form a distinct order of government with their jurisdiction defined; and

The Penner Report recommended Indian self-government.

3. While the Committee has concluded that the surest way to lasting change is through constitutional amendments, it encourages both the federal government and Indian First Nations to pursue all processes leading to the implementation of self-government.

The committee recommended over fifty changes in legislation and policy in such areas as membership, democratic criteria for self-government decisions within communities, scope of powers, economic foundations, financial arrangements, and lands and resources. The Penner Report was supported by Indian representatives and became a basis for future discussion and policy development in the 1980s.

Some governmental representatives, however, were concerned about a distinct order of government. They thought it would mean a third order of government with similar powers to provincial governments.

Some Indian First Nations wanted to move quickly to establish self-governing arrangements with Canada. In 1984, the Cree Naskapi of Quebec Act (for Cree peoples of northern Quebec) was passed by Parliament. It represented the first piece of Indian self-government legislation in Canada. This legislation contained some governmental arrangements, which are comparable to local and regional governments in Canada. It also

contained some unique aspects. There were provisions related to game harvesting and management, and environmental and family law. These are normally handled by provincial governments.

In 1986, the Sechelt Band on the west coast of British Columbia also acquired a form of self-government. This was done through new federal legislation and complementary provincial legislation. This agreement also broke new ground. It involved delegated legislative authority from both the federal and British Columbia governments in such areas as education, health and child welfare. These are also areas which are normally provincial responsibilities. Some Indian nations felt that this agreement did not go far enough in terms of the range of powers required. They felt it was too close to the municipal government model used elsewhere in Canada.

Both pieces of pioneering legislation for Cree Naskapi and Sechelt did accomplish, however, several new principles. Both groups have new powers of Indian government unique in Canada. They are no longer subject to the operation of the federal Indian Act because their authority now flows from legislation specifically negotiated and tailor-made for their own communities.

In 1986, the federal government developed a new policy on Indian self-government in response to the pressure for a new basis for negotiations. This policy acknowledged and supported some of the longer-term Penner recommendations such as constitutional self-government. It also provided different routes for Indian bands to follow in the shorter term. Bands should explore possibilities inside and outside of the Indian Act, depending upon the individual Indian community plans. The Sechelt Act is an example of this approach because it went beyond the Indian Act and allows the community to operate without the Indian Act restrictions.

Another area of federal policy change related to whether or not self-government could be included in comprehensive aboriginal rights claims.

In 1986, a government task force recommended that the self-government issues be included in the negotiations:

> . . . a new feature of the policy will be to allow for negotiation of a broader range of self-government matters. Such negotiations would need to :
> • Be consistent with the government's policy on Indian/Inuit community-based self-government.
> • Respect existing constitutional principles and government practice.
> • Take account of directions north of 60 toward public government and [surrender of power to Indian peoples by the federal government].[4]

The last point takes into account concerns of the governments of the Yukon and the Northwest Territories to have their own provincial status. This also was an issue in Meech

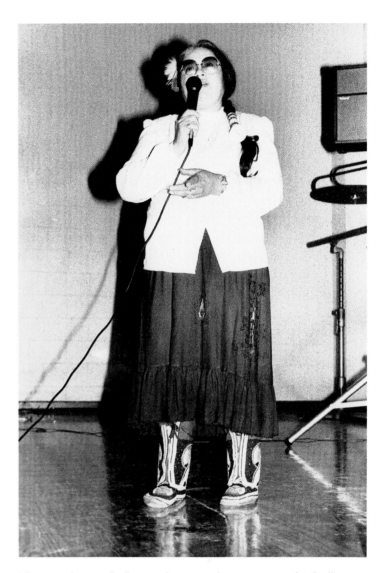

More and more Indian nations continue to press for Indian self-government.

Lake discussions. The federal policy did not, however, deal with constitutional inclusion of self-government as part of the land claims process for modern treaties. The policy is clear that this constitutionalizing of Indian self-government can only happen using the constitutional amendment process through First Ministers' Conferences.

Other Indian First Nations have followed the process started by Cree Naskapi and Sechelt communities. They have begun to work with the federal government to develop new legislation for themselves. By early 1990, about twenty of the more than 500 Indian First Nations across Canada were in the process of negotiating self-government arrangements with the government.

Others have begun simply to assert various self-governing practices based on what they consider their own authority. These include traditional forms of governing, such as the potlatch system of Indian decision-making of some Indian community councils in British Columbia.

Still other communities continue under various forms of Indian Affairs supervision. There are still a few Indian schools and programs run by Indian Affairs. These communities do not wish to take over the responsibilities.

Some communities are pressing for policies that more closely reflect their own views of inherent rights to self-government.

Academics have also developed several theories of Indian self-government. These theories introduce a variety of approaches: legal delegated, inherent rights, and political-institutional based approaches. Another way of thinking has been expressed as a well-being approach, which "concentrates on qualities of life that make it better, rather than worse."[5]

There are a whole range of theories, plans and practices in evidence. Indeed, this whole area of Indian self-government continues to be very dynamic and subject to change.

New generations of Indian leaders are calling upon their communities to try new avenues of self-determination. Sometimes, older community members are urging caution for a variety of reasons.

The processes for discussion and decision-making of these issues within Indian communities are probably just as important, if not more important than negotiations with government. Therefore, Indian self-government will remain a key topic for discussion in the decades to come.

Sharing Ideas

1. Explain clearly and thoroughly what is meant by the term "self-determination."

2. Explain what is meant by Indian self-government and why do Indian people want it.

3. Why was the term "band" replaced by the term "nation" in some Indian communities?

4. Identify who is represented in the following organizations:
   a) the Assembly of First Nations, and
   b) Prairie Treaty Nations Alliances

5. Outline why the prairie Indians separated from their national organization.

6. Distinguish between inherent rights and delegated rights.

Investigating Issues

1. Summarize advantages and disadvantages for Indian communities if they discard the Indian Act and establish self-government.

2. Examine the broad implications which the recommendations of the Penner Report would have on future negotiations regarding Indian self-government.

Key Words

Criteria Standards for making a judgement.

Delegate To entrust to another.

First Nations The Indian people and their descendants.

Inherent The essential character of something.

Why is Indian control of Indian education important?

A significant step forward in joint Indian and federal policy-making occurred in 1973.

In that year, the National Indian Brotherhood (now the Alliance of First Nations) presented a proposal on Indian Control of Indian Education to the government. Federal Minister of Indian Affairs Jean Chrétien agreed to the major components of the policy.

The key elements of the policy were:

1. Indian parents must have full responsibility and control of education; and
2. Band councils should be given total or partial authority for education on reserves.

This policy brought in a new era of Indian takeovers of federal schools on reserves. The number of band-operated schools increased from 53 in 1975 to 243 in 1986. If this trend continues, almost all schools on Indian reserves in Canada will shift from federal to Indian control.

One problem with implementation of the policy has been the lack of long-term financial planning by the government. Often the significant costs over and above teachers' salaries, such as new Native curriculum and special counselling needs, were neglected in the planning process.

Indian bands were sometimes expected to develop and manage schools without sufficient funds:

The most serious problem arises out of a lack of legislation. The Indian Act provides no direct legal basis for the transfer of control of education from the Minister to Indian bands. It authorizes the Minister to enter into agreements with provincial and territorial governments, public or separate school boards, or religious or charitable organizations, but not with Indian bands.[6]

The Sechelt Band in British Columbia overcame this problem of legislation by negotiating their own self-

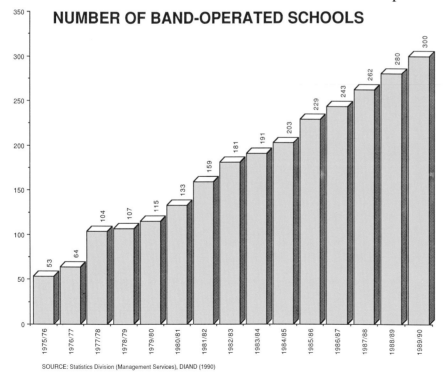

NUMBER OF BAND-OPERATED SCHOOLS

SOURCE: Statistics Division (Management Services), DIAND (1990)

116

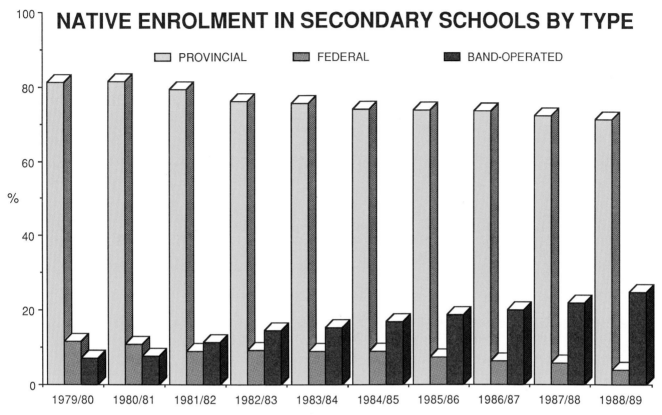

NATIVE ENROLMENT IN SECONDARY SCHOOLS BY TYPE

PROVINCIAL   FEDERAL   BAND-OPERATED

SOURCE: Education Branch, Indian and Inuit Affairs Program (1989)

government legislation. Nevertheless, for most Indian communities, the Indian Act problems remain.

Another controversy has developed over per student funding formulas for students in Indian-controlled schools. The federal government is trying to reduce its deficit. It wants to keep spending down. At the same time, Indian bands are seeking more money for their schools.

The federal government and the Indian communities are, however, working together to provide better facilities and more money for special programs.

117

UNIT 3

Sharing Ideas

1. Describe two major aspects of the National Indian Brotherhood education policy.

2. What difficulties did Indian bands encounter when given the responsibility of managing their own schools?

3. Distinguish between "control" over Indian education and "responsibility" for Indian education.

4. Suggest a role for the federal government regarding Indian education in the future.

Investigating Issues

1. Explain why control of education is so important to Indian communities.

2. Research how Indian education is controlled in your area. Outline the degree of band involvement, as well as federal and provincial government involvement.

3. What problems will Indian governments have to overcome in the area of Indian education?

Key Words

Deficit The amount by which a sum of money made falls short of the amount of money spent.

Is post-secondary education a treaty right?

Federal-Indian conflicts are not confined to schools on reserves. The increasing numbers of Indian students in higher education are causing another area of disagreement.

In 1978, Indian Affairs Minister Hugh Faulkner proposed that Indian post-secondary educational costs, such as tuition, books and living expenses, become a mandatory, or required, area of expenditure. Any qualified student who moved onto higher education would be eligible for funding support. Over the next decade, the numbers of Indian and Inuit students going to college and university increased dramatically.

A number of factors have contributed to this increase:
a) Indian leaders and organizations have pressed for more attention to Indian education;
b) The policy of "Indian Control of Indian Education" and the increasing number of band-operated schools and post-secondary transfer programs;

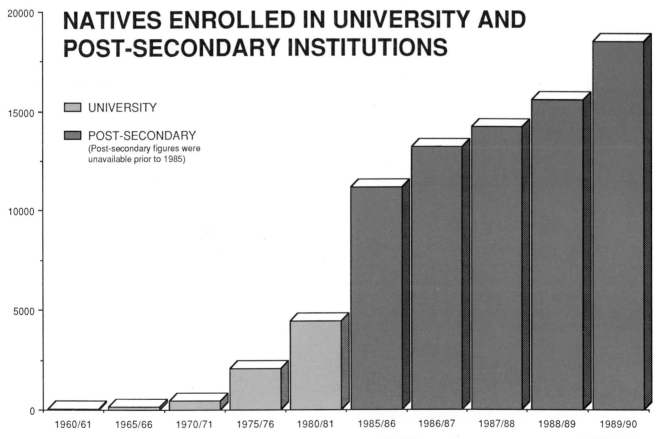

NATIVES ENROLLED IN UNIVERSITY AND POST-SECONDARY INSTITUTIONS

UNIVERSITY

POST-SECONDARY
(Post-secondary figures were unavailable prior to 1985)

1960/61 1965/66 1970/71 1975/76 1980/81 1985/86 1986/87 1987/88 1988/89 1989/90

SOURCE: Statistics Division and Educational Branch, DIAND (1990)

c) Growth of Native Studies programs in schools and at universities;
d) Special access programs were started in university faculties such as law, education and social work; and
e) Special counselling and financial assistance programs available to individual students.

Indian nations see post-secondary education as a treaty right.

In many university programs, over two-thirds of post-secondary Indian students are women. They are also increasingly moving into managerial and highly-skilled employment in the Indian communities and elsewhere.

In the future, these educated Indian women will play a significant role within the communities.

In 1988, a new Minister of Indian Affairs, William McKnight, said that open-ended access to post-secondary education must stop. The costs were rising too rapidly. Funding had risen from $52.9 million in 1984/85 to $121.9 million in 1988/89. There was also concern that the funding should have brought better results, such as more graduating Indian students.

In 1989, another new Minister of Indian Affairs, Pierre Cadieux, announced a new, more restricted access to post-secondary education.

This announcement produced a storm of protest across the country. Indian students in Ottawa went on a hunger strike for almost one month. Public pressure mounted, and the government provided funds to Indian organizations to propose new policies and processes.

A Parliamentary Standing Committee on Aboriginal Affairs made nine recommendations regarding the Post-Secondary Student Assistance Program, including:

1. ... an ongoing, full and meaningful consultation process be established between the Government of Canada and

aboriginal people. [On this issue the primary goal is] to reach a consensus on post-secondary policies and guidelines.

2. [Since the government] is clearly not in a position to decide the . . . legal issue of whether or not post-secondary education is a treaty right, [a forum jointly designed and mutually agreed to should] be created to resolve this fundamental disagreement between the Government of Canada and the treaty peoples.

3. [That] the program provide funding to each eligible applicant in each year.

4. That the long-term goal of the department [of Indian Affairs] should be to turn over management of the program to the aboriginal people.

Even though the Minister of Indian Affairs made some changes to the policy, most of these issues still remain.

For most of the Indian organizations, the key issue revolves around the principle of "education as a treaty and aboriginal right."

Some new steps have been taken. The Indian Affairs minister and the Saskatchewan Indian Nations signed a memorandum of agreement in 1989. This established a bilateral process on the treaties. They agreed to establish the Office of a Treaty Commissioner. This office would direct the process of resolving treaty issues, and would make recommendations to the minister and the treaty Indians. Both the federal government and the Saskatchewan Indians agreed that the two areas demanding immediate attention are land entitlement and education.

Later in 1989, Cliff Wright, a former mayor of Saskatoon, was appointed as the new commissioner. Chief Crowe's comment on the new treaty commissioner was:

Mr. Wright is a well-respected member of the Saskatchewan community and we are looking forward to working with him to resolve the outstanding treaty issues in the province.[7]

The Department of Indian Affairs has stated that the treaty right to education is confined to elementary and secondary education. On the other hand, Indian bands believe that post-secondary education is a treaty right. They are not asking for free education. In fact, Indian peoples do not view anything received from the treaties as being free. These rights, in their view, are prepaid. They feel these rights were agreed to during treaty negotiations.

University education as a treaty right will remain a controversial subject in the 1990s and beyond.

Sharing Ideas

1. List the factors that encouraged Indian students to seek higher education.

2. Identify what financial incentive further promoted post-secondary education.

3. Describe the view concerning funding for post-secondary education of:
   a) the Indian people, and
   b) the federal government.

4. Explain why Indian women are obtaining more of the managerial and professional jobs.

Investigating Issues

1. Do you perceive post-secondary education as a treaty right and/or an aboriginal right?

2. Review the negotiations involved in Treaty Eight (in Chapter 2) regarding the understanding of Laird and Kinosayoo on education. Record Laird's view and Kinosayoo's view.

3. Speculate on what changes will likely come to Indian communities if the percentage of university-educated Indian men and women continues to rise.

Key Words

Mandatory An obligation or command.

Memorandum of Agreement A written record of some issue or arrangement that concerns two or more governments.

Post-secondary transfer program Partial programs begun in one institution or school which can be carried on in a post-secondary institution or school.

Chapter 6
Treaty Relationship Renewal

In my mind, the key to the resolution of treaty problems is to look to the spirit of the Indian treaties. If the issues are approached this way, I think that we will find that while there is substantial disagreement about what the government was legally bound to provide, there is very good potential for agreement in terms of what the government might, in fact, provide in way of development assistance today.

– Lloyd Barber
Commissioner of Indian Claims for Canada, 1976

How will treaty and aboriginal rights issues be resolved in Canada?

The birth of Indian political organizations in the 1920s resulted in treaty rights concerns being presented to Parliament in the late 1940s. It was not until the 1970s and 1980s, however, that significant progress was made in resolving outstanding concerns about treaty rights.

In the last two decades, the federal and provincial governments, and Indian First Nations have struggled to find ways of resolving these concerns.

Common processes used by federal and provincial governments include:

1. Negotiating committees, with negotiators appointed by all parties in the dispute;
2. Indian claims commissioners appointed by the federal government;
3. First Ministers' Conferences on treaty and aboriginal rights, with elected federal, provincial and aboriginal leaders;
4. Parliamentary committees with Members of Parliament appointed by the government; and
5. Task forces with a team of public officials and/or private consultants to investigate a situation and come forward with recommendations.

Some processes have been conducted and initiated by Indian First Nations peoples themselves. These have often proven to be a useful forum for treaty rights issues.

At the international level, Canadian Indians have used the United Nations (UN) to bring forward treaty rights concerns. A recent UN statement was developed which involved a study of Indian treaties by an independent UN representative. As well, there are drafts of new UN understandings dealing with "Indigenous and Tribal Peoples in Independent Countries."

Earlier in this century, the highest Canadian courts seemed to water down or diminish the strength of the treaties. Therefore, these court interpretations of Indian treaties have a definite impact on peoples lives and the policies of governments.

Recent Supreme Court of Canada decisions have strengthened the legal position of the treaties in Canadian law in terms of some Indian understandings of the treaties.

One recent court decision in the British Columbia Court of Appeal provided the following modern principles of interpretation for Indian treaties in Canada:

1. Treaties should be given a fair, large and liberal construction in favour of the Indians;
2. Treaties must be construed not according to the technical meaning of the words, but in the sense that they would be naturally understood by the Indians;
3. As the honour of the Crown is always involved, no appearance of 'sharp dealing' should be sanctioned;

4. Any ambiguity in wording should be interpreted to the prejudice of the Indians if another construction is reasonably possible; and

5. Evidence by conduct or otherwise as to how the parties understood the treaty is of assistance in giving it content.[1]

Recent decisions of the Supreme Court of Canada affirm these more flexible, generous principles of treaty interpretation. Courts in the coming years will be called upon to interpret Indian treaties and more clearly define the legal meaning of Indian treaty rights. It must be kept in mind that the courts are part of a dynamic historical process. The courts are influenced by a variety of matters such as the quality of research done into the historical issues of Indian treaties.

One of the constant factors in treaty rights and Indian land claims issues is politics. It has been described this way:

> You are dealing with political issues. They are public issues where everyone feels he has, if not a direct interest, at least a sufficient interest to entitle him to have views on the subject and, more

Public opinion is important in resolving treaty issues.

A Mohawk and Canadian army infantryman stand face to face during a confrontation near Oka, Quebec.

extensive the legal arguments that may be made on behalf of the natives), the settlement of native claims will be determined by the political acceptance of their contents. What the government offers and finally negotiates must be acceptable to the public.[2]

Public opinion is therefore a vital factor in all settlements of Indian claims and grievances. Sometimes getting attention and starting processes for resolution of land claims or other grievances is difficult.

Indian First Nations have had to draw public attention to their concerns through such actions as:

1. Civil Disobedience: blockading public roads and stopping traffic without the legal authority to do so, engaging in "sit-ins" in departmental offices of government;
2. Public demonstrations by Indian peoples to protest government actions; and
3. Taking outstanding issues to the court systems of Canada.

often than not, views which he considers just and which should prevail. No matter how much the Native parties may ask for and no matter how little governments are willing to concede (and I would even go so far as to say that no matter how

Sharing Ideas

1. State one of the tactics that have been used by Indian First Nations to bring attention to their concerns.

2. Explain why the view of the public is instrumental in resolving disputes.

3. List the processes that have been used by the federal and provincial governments and the Indian peoples to resolve grievances or present issues.

4. In what ways have the public expressed sympathy with the Native cause?

5. How have non-Native lobby groups tried to influence the government's Indian policies?

Investigating Issues

1. Should Native people take action to advance their cause? What action would you recommend?

2. Is civil disobedience (defying the law) by the Indian peoples of Canada justified to advance their cause?

3. Should the Indians of Canada resort to armed struggle to advance their cause?

4. Discuss the implications of actions such as those taken by the Lubicon in northern Alberta (1988) and the Mohawks near Oka, Quebec in 1990.

5. Identify current cases of Indian action/reaction to government policy in land claim cases in your area.

Key Words

Ambiguity The possibility of two or more meanings to the same thing.

Indian Claims Commissioner A senior official appointed to investigate and report on Indian claims.

Task Force A group of people appointed to investigate or report on a given task.

What negotiating approaches have been effective, and what values and relationships must be considered?

As we seek bridges for the transition into the 1990s, the negotiating experience from elsewhere may be helpful. Harvard University's Negotiating Project has developed a theory based on successful negotiation experiences in a variety of conflict situations from all over the world. Titled "Principled Negotiation" or "Negotiations on Merits," it contains the following key points:

- Participants are problem-solvers.
- The goal is a wise outcome reached efficiently and amicably.
- *Separate the people from the problem.*
- Be soft on the people, hard on the problem.
- Proceed independent of trust.
- *Focus on interests, not positions.*
- Explore interests.
- Avoid having a bottom line.
- *Invent options for mutual gain.*
- Develop multiple options to choose from; decide later.
- *Insist on using objective criteria.*
- Try to reach a result based on standards independent of will.
- Reason and be open to reasons; yield to principle, not to pressure.[3]

As we reflect on this approach, the question arises — what might constitute objective criteria for negotiations? One way to think about the criteria might be to consider the importance of maintaining and renewing relationships between Canadians and Indian peoples.

Perhaps a more useful approach would be to consider our common values as Canadians. The treaty and aboriginal rights section of the constitution could be interpreted using the historical relationship of the Indian peoples to the land:

First, basic historical commitments made to native peoples should not be lightly overturned, and generally not without their consent . . . The commitments at times may have been ill considered . . . but they are the basis on which native peoples entered Canadian society and which gave them a stable foothold in an often difficult struggle to survive. If these commitments are now to be changed, native people must be fully involved in the process of renegotiation. Second, native people are not just people who happen to have a heritage different than the majority of Canadians . . . In many ways that one may not fully recognize or appreciate, Native Canadians represent our society's only deep historical links to the land, established over millennia. If their land is now our land as well, their relationship with that land is particularly worthy of understanding and respect.[4]

We must reflect on these fundamental values, in combination with the environmental concerns of all citizens everywhere, to ensure global survival. Perhaps we can rediscover both the original intent of treaty agreements and our common interests as a Canadian society.

Harold Cardinal expressed it this way:

Our elders had hoped to define a relationship in which both parties would not only share the wealth and resources of the country, but also the responsibility for utilizing those resources for the benefit of future generations.[5]

Sharing Ideas

1. Could the concern over the environment and land be a unifying value for the future of Native and non-Native Canadians? Comment on the view of environmental concerns and Native values.

2. Identify some of the common interests of Canadians, both Native and non-Native, as we strive to develop a more just and tolerant society for the future.

Investigating Issues

1. Review the chart below and suggest a negotiating approach which you would recommend to resolve outstanding issues. Should Native Canadians use a negotiating strategy or legal avenues to address concerns? Debate the advantages and disadvantages of each approach.

NEGOTIATION	LITIGATION
Pro	**Pro**
• wider range of issues can be reviewed	• final decisions can be made by higher courts in certain limited areas
• all key parties can be directly involved	
• agreements can produce "win-win" solutions for all parties	
Con	**Con**
• often very difficult to get all parties to the bargaining table	• lengthy process
• sometimes very hard to find common ground because of widely-divergent positions among parties	• costly for everyone
	• adversarial nature leads to tense relationships

Key Words

Amicably In a peaceful or friendly manner.

Millennium A period of a thousand years.

Theory A probable explanation based on observation and reasoning on the way things work.

Why does Canada need a Royal Commission on Native issues?

There have been many studies conducted and reports written in the 1970s and 1980s about ways of thinking and processes to resolve treaty rights grievances. For example, Indian Claims Commissioner Lloyd Barber stated in 1976:

> In my mind, the key to the resolution of treaty problems is to look to the spirit of the Indian treaties. If the issues are approached this way, I think that we will find that while there is substantial disagreement about what the government was legally bound to provide, there is very good potential for agreement in terms of what the government might, in fact, provide in way of development assistance today.[6]

What this suggests is that we put the legal issues on hold until we can regain a sense of the spirit or intent of the treaties.

One of the more important Royal Commissions of the 1970s — the MacKenzie River Valley Pipeline Inquiry of Justice Thomas Berger — was conducted into the impact of the pipeline on Native land claims and the environment. Berger recommended to Parliament a ten-year moratorium on the pipeline until claims were settled.

After an exhaustive study by a team of Native and non-Native lawyers, the Canadian Bar Association in 1989 made several recommendations in regard to treaty issues. In their report, they make the point that a new condition or environment is required if we are to overcome the bitterness that has developed over the failure to resolve treaty rights problems. In terms of concrete recommendations they suggest:

> A Royal Commission should be established to examine, study and report on treaty issues. The terms of reference and the membership of the commission should be agreed to by the parties. The terms of reference should include the task of devising a treaty modernization or implementation process that will take into account the "spirit and intent" of treaties as solemn and binding agreements.[7]

Perhaps a Royal Commission could be more broadly defined than simply just focusing on treaty rights. The hopes and dreams of Indian communities relate to a wide range

A Royal Commission makes recommendations to Parliament.

of social, economic, legal and
political matters.

To broaden the discussion further
in relation to Native issues, the
following questions may be helpful:

- Do we need better ways to
  discuss and resolve these
  issues as Canadians,
  community to community,
  person to person, instead of
  setting up costly Royal
  Commissions?
- Should we negotiate and talk
  instead of going to court or
  setting up blockades to get
  attention?

Specifically, a set of questions
revolves around the question of
current and future responsibilities of
both Native and non-Native
Canadians. For example:

1. Can we overcome the
   tendency of having to blame
   someone else?
2. Should we get on with our
   responsibilities as Canadians
   to build a firmer foundation
   for our children and
   grandchildren?
3. Do we lose our sense of
   balance and creativity or let
   our minds become locked into
   images from earlier times
   (for example, the Indian Act
   domination of Native peoples
   or stereotypes)?
4. Can we overcome these
   memories of the past, whether
   they be bitterness or
   stereotypes and fashion
   together a common vision for
   the future in Canada?
5. Do these responsibilities fall

to both young, old and the
middle generation from both
Native and non-Native
communities?

6. If we neglect these
   responsibilities, will the
   future generations pay the
   price in terms of violent
   confrontations?

Points to consider can be found
in a recent report of the federal
government's Parliamentary
Committee on Aboriginal Affairs.
The 1990 report covered a wide
range of thirty issues from land
claims to literacy. Canada's
parliamentarians concluded:

> The lack of knowledge Canadians
> generally have concerning the culture,
> history and aspirations of aboriginal
> peoples is an indication of the extent of
> the work that remains to be done. The
> circle of Confederation will not be
> complete until the social, economic
> and political marginalization of
> Canada's aboriginal people is
> reversed.[8]

A Supreme Court of Canada
decision has stressed the importance
of the relationship:

> The relationship between the
> government and aboriginals is
> trust-like, rather than adversarial, and
> contemporary recognition and
> affirmation of aboriginal rights must
> be defined in light of this historic
> relationship . . .[9]

Hopefully, this look at the
Canadian legacy has made a small
contribution to those educational
goals through an increased
understanding of Indian treaty
relationships.

131

UNIT 3

Sharing Ideas

1. Explain what is meant by "the spirit and the intent" of the treaties.
2. Do we need a Royal Commission on Native issues? Defend your position.

Investigating Issues

1. Should the numbered treaties of the last century be translated into modern terms so that there is a common understanding today? Develop a rationale for interpreting the treaties in modern terms.
2. Identify current Native issues in your area, and suggest a resolution to these issues by using a negotiating strategy.

Key Words

Marginal Barely useful or acceptable.

Moratorium A pause in action on an issue.

Royal Commission An official inquiry appointed by Parliament to look into matters of public concern.

Epilogue

One does not reach this age merely to think of the past, but to have hope and aspirations for the future, and to do something so history and a way of life may continue for the purpose it was intended.

— Alexander Wolfe

As Canada embarks on the decade of the 1990s, there are four questions which may be useful to keep in mind in the search for new (or different) solutions to difficult issues:

1. *What has been learned from past and present Indian leaders about the importance of respectful relationships?*

This stress on relationships of mutual respect and sharing of the bountiful resources of this land of Canada has been an ongoing theme of Indian leaders in Canada — west and east.

The 500th anniversary of Columbus' "discovery" of North America is in 1992. Many North Americans see this as an occasion to celebrate. Native North Americans are much less certain that there is much to celebrate.

Canada's future generations receive a mixed legacy. One legacy is that of broken treaty promises (or failure to fully implement treaties). Yet, there is also a positive legacy of mutual respect and cooperation gained from the original spirit of the treaty negotiations, and the partial fulfillment of treaty promises.

Thus, there are aspects of our history which are well-suited to building more harmonious relationships as a legacy for future generations.

2. *Is it possible to develop a more inclusive and unified Canadian society?*

In the 1990s, a number of important decisions are being presented to Canadians. These matters concern the nature of Canada, its constitution and its future. What will Quebec's position be in Canada? What will Quebec and the rest of Canada decide to do about our constitution and basic institutions of government?

Aboriginal Canadians and other Canadians will also have other choices to make. The federal government's Spicer Commission has included the following questions in its twelve key discussion points:

   a)   What are your views on the relationship between Canada's aboriginal and non-aboriginal peoples?

   b)   What are your views on settling aboriginal land claims?

134

c) What do you think the effect of aboriginal self-government would be on:
   i)   aboriginal communities?
   ii) Canada?[1]

Other questions are posed by provincial governments or their
representatives:

How are smaller reserves, if recognized as individual nations, to do all that
governments do, given the limited dollars available to them?[2]

Should guaranteed seats be provided to aboriginal peoples in the House of Commons,
the Senate and provincial legislatures?[3]

One thing is certain — the views of aboriginal Canadians will be
presented eloquently and with emotion. Andrew Bear Robe, Constitutional
Advisor to the Siksika Nation, put it this way — "Our aspirations are no less
significant or less intense than those of Quebec."

3. *How can Canadians keep abreast of the rapidly changing current
   affairs?*

The Throne Speech for Parliament in May, 1991, contained the
announcement that the Rt. Honourable Brian Dickson has been asked by the
Prime Minister of Canada to recommend terms of reference and composition
of a *Royal Commission on Aboriginal Peoples in Canada*. Also in May,
1991, the Parliamentary Committee on Aboriginal Affairs made a report on
The Summer of 1990, and its recommendations included such matters as a
needed Royal Commission, a review of the national Defense Act, and a
better system for resolving land claims disputes.

These changing times challenge all of us to continue to keep informed —
an ongoing citizenship responsibility.

4. *What is the advice of elderly Canadians about the difficult times we are
   encountering in Canada?*

The experience and wisdom of elderly citizens provides all Canadians
with an important human resource that should be included in the important
decision-making process of the 1990s.

All these things we have, and from there we should be able to talk about the discovery of things the white man wrote about our treaties. He wrote his treaties from his understanding and we wrote ours from our understanding. When we go back to the point of the original men with the Indian and the white, they were made by the same Creator; the Creator who made both these people was kind. Because He was a Creator and He was Good, He dealt with both the original men with peace and fairness, so that neither of the original men would have anything to be unsatisfied about . . . The other thing we should keep in mind is that since the Creator dealt fairly with both the original men, and since He tried to make them both equally happy, we also have a responsibility today, whatever we come up with, to make sure that both sides are happy. I would be particularly pleased if the young people would fully understand what this all means. [4]

Appendix
Sample of a Treaty ━━━━━━━━━━━━━━━━━━━━━━━━━━━

REPORT OF
COMMISSIONERS FOR TREATY No. 8
WINNIPEG, MANITOBA, 22nd September, 1899.

The Honourable
> CLIFFORD SIFTON,
>> Superintendent General of Indian Affairs,
>>> Ottawa.

SIR, — We have the honour to transmit herewith the treaty which, under the Commission issued to us on the 6th day of April last, we have made with the Indians of the provisional district of Athabasca and parts of the country adjacent thereto, as described in the treaty and shown on the map attached.

The date fixed for meeting the Indians at Lesser Slave Lake was the 8th of June, 1899. Owing, however, to unfavourable weather and lack of boatmen, we did not reach the point until the 19th. But one of the Commissioners — Mr. Ross — who went overland from Edmonton to the Lake, was fortunately present when the Indians first gathered. He was thus able to counteract the consequences of the delay and to expedite the work of the Commission by preliminary explanations of its objects.

We met the Indians on the 20th, and on the 21st the treaty was signed.

As the discussions at the different points followed on much the same lines, we shall confine ourselves to a general statement of their import. There was a marked absence of the old Indian style of oratory. Only among the Wood Crees were any formal speeches made, and these were brief. The Beaver Indians are taciturn. The Chipewyans confined themselves to asking questions and making brief arguments. They appeared to be more adept at cross-examination than at speech-making, and the Chief at Fort Chipewyan displayed considerable keenness of intellect and much practical sense in pressing the claims of his band. They all wanted as liberal, if not more liberal terms, than were granted to the Indians of the plains. Some expected to be fed by the Government after the making of treaty, and all asked for assistance in seasons of distress and urged that the old and indigent who were no longer able to hunt and trap and were consequently often in distress should be cared for by the Government. They requested that medicines be furnished. At Vermilion, Chipewyan and Smith's Landing, an earnest appeal was made for the services of a medical man. There was expressed at every point the fear that the making of the treaty would be followed by the curtailment of the hunting and fishing privileges, and many were impressed with the notion that the treaty would lead to taxation and enforced military service. They seemed desirous of securing educational advantages for their children, but stipulated that in the matter of schools there should be no interference with their religious beliefs.

We pointed out that the Government could not undertake to maintain Indians in idleness; that the same means of earning a livelihood would continue after the treaty as existed before it, and that the Indians would be expected to make use of them. We told them that the Government was always ready to give relief in cases of actual destitution, and that in seasons of distress they would without any special stipulation in the treaty receive such assistance as was usual to give in order to prevent starvation among Indians in any part of Canada; and we stated that the attention of the Government would be called to the need of some special provision being made for assisting the old and indigent who were unable to work and dependent on charity for the means of sustaining life. We promised that supplies of medicines would be put in the charge of persons selected by the Government at different points, and would be distributed free to those of the Indians who might require them. We explained that it would be practically impossible for the Government to arrange for regular medical attendance upon Indians so widely scattered over such an extensive territory. We assured them, however, that the Government would always be ready to avail itself of any opportunity of affording medical service just as it provided that the physician attached to the Commission should give free attendance to all Indians whom he might find in need of treatment as he passed through the country.

Our chief difficulty was the apprehension that the hunting and fishing privileges were to be curtailed. The provision in the treaty under which ammunition and twine is to be furnished went far in the direction of quieting the fears of the Indians, for they admitted that it would be unreasonable to furnish the means of hunting and fishing if laws were to be enacted which would make hunting and fishing so restricted as to render it impossible to make a livelihood by such pursuits. But over and above the provision, we had to solemnly assure them that only such laws as to hunting and fishing as were in the interest of the Indians and were found necessary in order to protect the fish and fur-bearing animals would be made, and that they would be as free to hunt and fish after the treaty as they would be if they never entered into it.

We assured them that the treaty would not lead to any forced interference with their mode of life, that it did not open the way to the imposition of any tax, and that there was no fear of enforced military service. We showed them that, whether treaty was made or not, they were subject to the law, bound to obey it, and liable to punishment for any infringements of it. We pointed out that the law was designed for the protection of all, and must be respected by all the inhabitants of the country, irrespective of colour or origin; and that, in requiring them to live at peace with white men who came into the country, and not to molest them in person or in property, it only required them to do what white men were required to do as to the Indians.

As to education, the Indians were assured that there was no need of any special stipulation, as it was the policy of the Government to provide in every part of the country, as far as circumstances would permit, for the education of Indian children, and that the law, which was as strong as a treaty, provided for non-interference with the religion of the Indians in schools maintained or assisted by the Government.

We should add that the chief of the Chipewyans of Fort Chipewyan asked that the Government should undertake to have a railway built into the country, as the cost of goods which the Indians require would be thereby cheapened and the prosperity of the country enhanced. He was told that the Commissioners had no authority to make any statement in the matter further than to say that his desire would be made known to the Government.

When we conferred, after the first meeting with the Indians at Lesser Slave Lake, we came to the conclusion that it would be best to make one treaty covering the whole of the territory ceded, and to take adhesions thereto from the Indians to be met at the other points rather than to make several separate treaties.

The treaty was therefore so drawn as to provide three ways in which assistance is to be given to the Indians, in order to accord with the conditions of the country and to meet the requirements of the Indians in the different parts of the territory.

In addition to the annuity, which we found it necessary to fix at the figures of Treaty Six, which covers adjacent territory, the treaty stipulates that assistance in the form of seed and implements and cattle will be given to those of the Indians who may take to farming, in the way of cattle and mowers to those who may devote themselves to cattle-raising, and that ammunition and twine will be given to those who continue to fish and hunt. The assistance in farming and ranching is only to be given when the Indians actually take to these pursuits, and it is not likely that for many years there will be a call for any considerable expenditure under these heads. The only Indians of the territory ceded who are likely to take to cattle-raising are those about Lesser Slave Lake and along the Peace River, where there is quite an extent of ranching country; and although there are stretches of cultivable land in those parts of the country, it is not probable that the Indians will, while present conditions obtain, engage in farming further than the raising of roots in a small way, as is now done to some extent. In the main the demand will be for ammunition and twine, as the great majority of the Indians will continue to hunt and fish for a livelihood. It does not appear likely that the conditions of the country on either side of the Athabasca and Slave Rivers or about Athabasca Lake will be so changed as to affect hunting or trapping, and it is safe to say that so long as the fur-bearing animals remain, the great bulk of the Indians will continue to hunt and to trap.

The Indians are given the option of taking reserves or land in severalty. As the extent of the country treated for made it impossible to define reserves or holdings, and as the Indians were not prepared to make selections, we confined ourselves to an undertaking to have reserves and holdings set apart in the future, and the Indians were satisfied with the promise that this would be done when required. There is no immediate necessity for the general laying out of reserves or the allotting of land. It will be quite time enough to do this as advancing settlement makes necessary the surveying of the land. Indeed, the Indians were generally averse to being placed on reserves. It would have been impossible to have made a treaty if we had not assured them that there was no intention of confining them to reserves. We had to very clearly explain to them that the provision for reserves and allotments of land were made for their protection, and to secure to them in perpetuity a fair portion of the land ceded, in the event of settlement advancing.

After making the treaty at Lesser Slave Lake it was decided that, in order to offset the delay already referred to, it would be necessary for the Commission to divide. Mr. Ross and Mr. McKenna accordingly set out for Fort St. John on the 22nd of June. The date appointed for meeting the Indians there was the 21st. When the decision to divide was come to, a special messenger was dispatched to the Fort with a message to the Indians explaining the delay, advising them that Commissioners were travelling to meet them, and requesting them to wait at the Fort. Unfortunately the Indians had dispersed and gone to their hunting grounds before the messenger arrived and weeks before the date originally fixed for the meeting, and when the Commissioners got within some miles of St. John the messenger met them with a letter from the Hudson's Bay Company's officer there advising them that the Indians after consuming all their provisions, set off on the 1st of June in four different bands and in as many different directions for the regular hunt; that there was not a man at St. John who knew the country and could carry word of the Commissioners' coming, and even if there were it would take three weeks or a month to get the Indians in. Of course there was nothing to do but return. It may be stated, however, that what happened was not altogether unforeseen. We had grave doubts of being able to get to St. John in time to meet the Indians, but as they were reported to be rather disturbed and ill-disposed on account of the actions of miners passing through their country, it was thought that it would be well to show them that the Commissioners were prepared to go into their country, and that they had put forth every possible effort to keep the engagement made by the Government.

The Commissioners on their return from St. John met the Beaver Indians of Dunvegan on the 21st day of June and secured their adhesion to the treaty. They then proceeded to Fort Chipewyan and to Smith's Landing on the Slave River and secured the adhesion of the Cree and Chipewyan Indians at these points on the 13th and 17th days of July respectively.

138

In the meantime Mr. Laird met the Cree and Beaver Indians at Peace River Landing and Vermilion, and secured their adhesion on the 1st and 8th days of July respectively. He then proceeded to Fond du Lac on Lake Athabasca, and obtained the adhesion of the Chipewyan Indians there on the 25th and 27th days of July.

After treating with the Indians at Smith, Mr. Ross and Mr. McKenna found it necessary to separate in order to make sure of meeting the Indians at Wabisca on the date fixed. Mr. McKenna accordingly went to Fort McMurray, where he secured the adhesion of the Chipewyan and Cree Indians on the 4th day of August, and Mr. Ross proceeded to Wabisca, where he obtained the adhesion of the Cree Indians on the 14th day of August.

The Indians with whom we treated differ in may respects from the Indians of the organized territories. They indulge in neither paint nor feathers, and never clothe themselves in blankets. Their dress is of the ordinary style and many of them were well clothed. In the summer they live in teepees, but many of them have log houses in which they live in winter. The Cree language is the chief language of trade, and some of the Beavers and Chipewyans speak it in addition to their own tongues. All the Indians we met were with rare exceptions professing Christians, and showed evidences of the work which missionaries have carried on among them for many years. A few of them have had their children avail themselves of the advantages afforded by boarding schools established at different missions. None of the tribes appear to have any very definite organization. They are held together mainly by the language bond. The chiefs and headmen are simply the most efficient hunters and trappers. They are not law-makers and leaders in the sense that the chiefs and headmen of the plains and of old Canada were. The tribes have no very distinctive characteristics, and as far as we could learn no traditions of any import. The Wood Crees are an off-shoot of the Crees of the South. The Beaver Indians bear some resemblance to the Indians west of the mountains. The Chipewyans are physically the superior tribe. The Beavers have apparently suffered most from scrofula and phthisis, and there are marks of these diseases more or less among all the tribes.

Although in manners and dress the Indians of the North are much further advanced in civilization than other Indians were when treaties were made with them, they stand as much in need of the protection afforded by the law to aborigines as do any other Indians of the country, and are as fit subjects for the paternal care of the Government.

It may be pointed out that hunting in the North differs from hunting as it was on the plains in that the Indians hunt in a wooded country and instead of moving in bands go individually or in family groups.

Our journey from point to point was so hurried that we are not in a position to give any description of the country ceded which would be of value. But we may say that about Lesser Slave Lake there are stretches of country which appear well suited for ranching and mixed farming; that on both sides of the Peace River there are extensive prairies and some well wooded country; that at Vermilion, on the Peace, two settlers have successfully carried on mixed farming on a pretty extensive scale for several years, and that the appearance of the cultivated fields of the Mission there in July showed that cereals roots were as well advanced as in any portion of the organized territories. The country along the Athabasca River is well wooded and there are miles of tar-saturated banks. But as far as our restricted view of the Lake Athabasca and Slave River country enabled us to judge, its wealth, apart from possible mineral development, consists exclusively in its fisheries and furs.

In going from Peace River Crossing to St. John, the trail which is being constructed under the supervision of the Territorial Government from moneys provided by Parliament was passed over. It was found to be well located. The grading and bridge work is of a permanent character, and the road is sure to be an important factor in the development of the country.

We desire to express our high appreciation of the valuable and most willing service rendered by Inspector Snyder and the corps of police under him, and at the same time to testify to the efficient manner in which the members of our staff performed their several duties. The presence of a medical man was much appreciated by the Indians, and Dr. West, the physician to the Commission, was most assiduous in attending to the great number of Indians who sought his services. We would add that the Very Reverend Father Lacombe, who was attached to the Commission, zealously assisted us in treating with the Crees.

The actual number of Indians paid was: —

7	Chiefs at $32	$224 00
23	Headmen at $22	$506 00
2,187	Indians at $12	$26,244 00
		$26,974 00

A detailed statement of the Indians treated with and of the money paid is appended.
We have the honour to be, sir,
Your obedient servants,
DAVID LAIRD,
J. H. ROSS,
J. A. J. McKENNA.
Indian Treaty Commissioners

TREATY No. 8.

ARTICLES OF A TREATY made and concluded at the several dates mentioned therein, in the year of Our Lord one thousand eight hundred and ninety-nine, between Her most Gracious Majesty the Queen of Great Britain and Ireland, by Her Commissioners the Honourable David Laird, of Winnipeg, Manitoba, Indian Commissioner for the said Province and the Northwest Territories; James Andrew Joseph McKenna, of Ottawa, Ontario, Esquire, and the Honourable James Hamilton Ross, of Regina, in the Northwest Territories, of the one part; and the Cree, Beaver, Chipewyan and other Indians, inhabitants of the territory within the limits hereinafter defined and described, by their Chiefs and Headmen, hereunto subscribed, of the other part:—

WHEREAS, the Indians inhabiting the territory hereinafter defined have, pursuant to notice given by the Honourable Superintendent General of Indian Affairs in the year 1898, been convened to meet a Commission representing Her Majesty's Government of the Dominion of Canada at certain places in the said territory in this present year 1899, to deliberate upon certain matters of interest to Her Most Gracious Majesty, of the one part, and the said Indians of the other.

AND WHEREAS, the said Indians have been notified and informed by Her Majesty's said Commission that it is Her desire to open for settlement, immigration, trade, travel, mining, lumbering, and such other purposes as to Her Majesty may seem meet, a tract of country bounded and described as herein- after mentioned, and to obtain the consent thereto of Her Indian subjects inhabiting the said tract, and to make a treaty, and arrange with them, so that there may be peace and good will between them and Her Majesty's other subjects, and that Her Indian people may know and be assured of what allowances they to count upon and receive from Her Majesty's bounty and benevolence.

AND WHEREAS, the Indians of the said tract, duly convened in council at the respective points named hereunder, and being requested by Her Majesty's Commissioners to name certain Chiefs and Headmen who should be authorized on their behalf to conduct such negotiations and sign any treaty to be founded thereon, and to become responsible to Her Majesty for the faithful performance by their respective bands of such obligations as shall be assumed by them, the said Indians have therefore acknowledged for that purpose the several Chiefs and Headmen who have subscribed hereto.

AND WHEREAS, the said Commissioners have proceeded to negotiate a treaty with the Cree, Beaver, Chipewyan and other Indians, inhabiting the district hereinafter defined and described, and the same has been agreed upon and concluded by the respective bands at the dates mentioned hereunder, the said Indians DO HEREBY CEDE, RELEASE, SURRENDER AND YIELD up to the Government of the Dominion of Canada, for Her Majesty the Queen and Her successors for ever, all their rights, titles and privileges whatsoever, to the lands included within the following limits, that is to say:—

Commencing at the source of the main branch of the Red Deer River in Alberta, thence due west to the central range of the Rocky Mountains, thence northwesterly along the said range to the point where it intersects the 60th parallel of north latitude, thence east along said parallel to the point where it intersects Hay River, thence northeasterly down said river to the south shore of Great Slave Lake, thence along the said shore northeasterly (and including such rights to the islands in said lakes as the Indians mentioned in the treaty may possess), and thence easterly and northeasterly along the south shores of Christie's Bay and McLeod's Bay to old Fort Reliance near the mouth of Lockhart's River, thence southeasterly in a straight line to and including Black Lake, thence southwesterly up the stream from Cree Lake, thence including said lake southwesterly along the height of land between the Athabasca and Churchill Rivers to where it intersects the northern boundary of Treaty Six, and along the said boundary easterly, northerly and southwesterly, to the place of commencement.

AND ALSO the said Indian rights, titles and privileges whatsoever to all other lands wherever situated in the Northwest Territories, British Columbia, or in any other portion of the Dominion of Canada.

To HAVE AND TO HOLD the same to Her Majesty the Queen and Her successors for ever.

And Her Majesty the Queen HEREBY AGREES with the said Indians that they shall have right to pursue their usual vocations of hunting, trapping and fishing throughout the tract surrendered as heretofore described, subject to such regulations as may from time to time be made by the Government of the country, acting under the authority of Her Majesty, and saving and excepting such tracts as may be required or taken up from time to time for settlement, mining, lumbering, trading or other purposes.

And Her Majesty the Queen hereby agrees and undertakes to lay aside reserves for such bands as desire reserves, the same not to exceed in all one square mile for each family of five for such number of families as may elect to reside on reserves, or in that proportion for larger or smaller families; and for such families or individual Indians as may prefer to live apart from band reserves, Her Majesty undertakes to provide land in severalty to the extent of 160 acres to each Indian, the land to be conveyed with a proviso as to non-alienation without the consent of the Governor General in Council of Canada, the selection of such reserves, and lands in severalty, to be made in the manner following, namely, the Superintendent General of Indian Affairs shall depute and send a suitable person to determine and set apart such reserves and lands, after consulting with the Indians concerned as to the locality which may be found suitable and open for selection.

Provided, however, that Her Majesty reserves the right to deal with any settlers within the bounds of any lands reserved for any band as She may see fit; and also that the aforesaid reserves of land, or any interest therein, may be sold or otherwise disposed of by Her Majesty's Government for the use and benefit of the said Indians entitled thereto, with their consent first had and obtained.

It is further agreed between Her Majesty and Her said Indian subjects that such portions of the reserves and lands above indicated as may at any time be required for public works, buildings, railways, or roads of whatsoever nature may be appropriated for that purpose by Her Majesty's Government of the Dominion of Canada, due compensation being made to the Indians for the value of any improvements thereon, and an equivalent in land, money or other consideration for the area of the reserve so appropriated.

And with a view to show the satisfaction of Her Majesty with the behaviour and good conduct of Her Indians- and in extinguishment of all their past claims, She hereby, through Her Commissioners, agrees to make each Chief a present of thirty-two dollars in cash, to each Headman twenty-two dollars, and to every other Indian of whatever age, of the families represented at the time and place of payment, twelve dollars.

Her Majesty also agrees that next year, and annually afterwards for ever, She will cause to be paid to the said Indians in cash, at suitable places and dates, of which the said Indians shall be duly notified, to each Chief twenty-five dollars, each Headman, not to exceed four to a large Band and two to a small Band, fifteen dollars, and to every other Indian, of whatever age, five dollars, the same, unless there be some exceptional reason, to be paid only to heads of families for those belonging thereto.

FURTHER, Her Majesty agrees that each Chief, after signing the treaty, shall receive a silver medal and a suitable flag, and next year, and every third year thereafter, each Chief and Headman shall receive a suitable suit of clothing.

FURTHER, Her Majesty agrees to pay the salaries of such teachers to instruct the children of said Indians as to Her Majesty's Government of Canada may seem advisable.

FURTHER, Her Majesty agrees to supply each Chief of a Band that selects a reserve, for the use of that Band, ten axes, five hand-saws, five augers, one grindstone, and the necessary files and whetstones.

FURTHER, Her Majesty agrees that each Band that elects to take a reserve and cultivate the soil, shall, as soon as convenient after such reserve is set aside and settled upon, and the Band has signified its choice and is prepared to break up the soil, receive two hoes, one spade, one scythe and two hay forks for every family so settled, and for every three families one plough and one harrow, and to the Chief, for the use of his Band, two horses or a yoke of oxen, and for each Band, potatoes, barley, oats and wheat (if such seed be suited to the locality of the reserve), to plant the land actually broken up, and provisions for one month in the spring for several years while planting such seeds; and to every family one cow, and every Chief one bull, and one mowing-machine and one reaper for the use of his Band when it is ready for them; for such families as prefer to raise stock instead of cultivating the soil, every family of five persons, two cows, and every Chief two bulls and two mowing-machines when ready for their use, and a like proportion for smaller or larger families. The aforesaid articles, machines and cattle to be given one for all for the encouragement of agriculture and stock raising; and for such Bands as prefer to continue hunting and fishing, as much ammunition and twine for making nets annually as will amount in value to one dollar per head of the families so engaged in hunting and fishing.

And the undersigned Cree, Beaver, Chipewyan and other Indian Chiefs and Headmen, on their own behalf and on behalf of all the Indians whom they represent, DO HEREBY SOLEMNLY PROMISE and engage to strictly observe this Treaty, and also to conduct and behave themselves as good and loyal subjects of Her Majesty the Queen.

THEY PROMISE AND ENGAGE that they will, in all respects, obey and abide by the law; that they will maintain peace between each other, and between themselves and other tribes of Indians, and between themselves and others of Her Majesty's subjects, whether Indians, half-breeds or whites, this year inhabiting and hereafter to inhabit any part of the said ceded territory; and that they will not molest the person or property of any inhabitant of such ceded tract, or of any other district or country, or interfere with or trouble any person passing or travelling through the said tract or any part thereof, and that they will assist the officers of Her Majesty in bringing to justice and punishment any Indian, offending against the stipulations of this Treaty or infringing the law in force in the country so ceded.

IN WITNESS WHEREOF Her Majesty's said Commissioners and the Cree Chief and Headmen of Lesser Slave Lake and the adjacent territory, HAVE HEREUNTO SET THEIR HANDS at Lesser Slave Lake on the twenty-first day of June, in the year herein first above written.

Signed by the parties hereto, in the presence of the undersigned witnesses, the same having been first explained to the Indians by Albert Tate and Samuel Cunningham, Interpreters.	DAVID LAIRD, *Treaty Commissioner,* J. A. J. MCKENNA, *Treaty Commissioner,* J. H. ROSS, *Treaty Commissioner,*
FATHER A. LACOMBE, GEO. HOLMES, E. GROUARD, W. G. WHITE, JAMES WALKER, J. ARTHUR COTE, A. E. SNYDER, INSP. N.W.M.P., H. B. ROUND, HARRISON S. YOUNG, J. F. PRUD'HOMME, J. W. MARTIN, C. MAIR, H. A. CONROY, PIERRE DESCHAMBEAULT, RICHARD SECORD, M. MCCAULEY.	KEE NOO SHAY OO, Chief, his X mark MOOSTOOS, Headman, his X mark FELIX GIROUX, Headman, his X mark WEE CHEE WAY, Headman, his X mark CHARLES NEE SUE TA SIS, Headman, his X mark CAPTAIN, Headman, from Sturgeon Lake. his X mark

IN WITNESS WHEREOF the Chairman of Her Majesty's Commissioners and the Headman of the Indians of Peace River Landing and the adjacent territory, in behalf of himself and the Indians whom he represents, have hereunto set their hands at the said Peace River Landing on the first day of July in the year of Our Lord one thousand eight hundred and ninety-nine.

Signed by the parties hereto, in the presence of the undersigned witnesses, the same having been first explained to the Indians by Father A. Lacombe and John Bourassa, Interpreters.

A. LACOMBE,
E. GROUARD, O.M.I., Ev. d'Ibora,
GEO. HOLMES,
HENRY McCORRISTER,
K. F. ANDERSON, Sgt., N.W.M.P.,
PIERRE DESCHAMBEAULT,
H. A. CONROY,
T. A. BRICK,
HARRISON S. YOUNG,
J. W. MARTIN,
DAVID CURRY.

DAVID LAIRD, *Treaty Commissioner,*

DUNCAN TASTAOOSTS, *Headman of the*
Crees,
his X mark

In witness whereof the Chairman of Her Majesty's Commissioners and the Chief and Headmen of the Beaver and Headman of the Crees and other Indians of Vermilion and the adjacent territory, in behalf of themselves and the Indians whom they represent, have hereunto set their hands at Vermilion on the eighth day of July, in the year of our Lord one thousand eight hundred and ninety-nine.

Signed by the parties hereto, in the presence of the undersigned witnesses, the same having been first explained to the Indians by Father A. Lacombe and John Bourassa, Interpreters.

A. LACOMBE,
E. GROUARD, O.M.I., Ev. d'Ibora,
GEO. HOLMES,
MALCOLM SCOTT,
F. D. WILSON, H. B. Co.,
H. A. CONROY,
PIERRE DESCHAMBEAULT,
HARRISON S. YOUNG,
J. W. MARTIN,
A. P. CLARKE,
CHAS. H. STUART WADE,
K. F. ANDERSON, Sgt., N.W.M.P.

DAVID LAIRD, *Treaty Commissioner,*

PIERROT FOURNIER, *Chief, Beaver*
Indians,
his X mark

KUIS KUIS KOW CA POOHOO, *Headman,*
Beaver Indians,
his X mark

In witness whereof the Chairman of Her Majesty's Treaty Commissioners and the Chief and Headman of the Chipewyan Indians of Fond du Lac (Lake Athabasca) and the adjacent territory, in behalf of themselves and the Indians whom they represent, have hereunto set their hands at the said Fond du Lac on the twenty-fifth and twenty-seventh days of July, in the year of Our Lord one thousand eight hundred and ninety-nine.

Notes

SECTION 1

1. Alexander Wolfe, *Earth Elder Stories*, p. xi.

2. Ibid. p. xii.

3. George Stanley in Getty, I.A.L. and A. S. Lassier, *As Long as the Sun Shines and Water Flows*, (University of British Columbia Press, 1983), p. 2.

CHAPTER ONE

1. Peter Elias, *The Dakota of the Canadian Northwest*, (University of Manitoba, Winnipeg, 1988), p. 29.

2. Supreme Court of Canada Judgement, Sioui case, (May, 1990), p. 29.

3. Supreme Court of Canada Judgement, Sioui case, (May, 1990), p. 18.

4. John Foster in Richard Price, ed., *The Spirit of the Alberta Indian Treaties*, (University of Alberta Press, Edmonton, 1987), p. 190.

5. Alexander Morris, *The Treaties of Canada with the Indians*, (Coles Publishing Co., 1971), [Reprint from original Bedford and Clarke Co., Toronto, 1880], p. 199.

6. Ibid. p. 272.

7. Ibid. p. 267.

8. Acton Burrows cited in Doug Owram, *Promise of Eden, The Canadian Expansionist Movement and the Idea of the West 1856-1900*, (University of Toronto Press, Toronto, 1980), p. 134.

9. Morris, *The Treaties of Canada with the Indians*, pp. 170-71.

10. Ibid, p. 171.

11. Stanley, *The Birth of Western Canada*, (University of Toronto Press, Toronto, 1962), pp. 275-76.

12. John Buffalo in R. Price. ed., *The Spirit of the Alberta Indian Treaties*, p. 119.

13. Lynn Hickey in R. Price. ed., *The Spirit of the Alberta Indian Treaties,*, p. 105.

14. Peter Erasmus, *Buffalo Days and Nights*, (Glenbow-Alberta Institute, 1976), p. 244.

15. Morris, *The Treaties of Canada with the Indians*, pp. 216-17.

CHAPTER TWO

1. Charles Mair, *Through the MacKenzie Basin: A Narrative of the Athabasca and Peace River Expedition of 1899*, (W. Briggs, Toronto, 1908), p. 23.

2. Ibid, p. 61.

3. Ibid, p. 62.

4. Ibid, pp. 62-63.

5. Treaty Eight Commissioner's Report, 1899, (Queen's Printer, 1966), p. 6.

CHAPTER THREE

1. Lazarus Roan in Richard Price, ed., *The Spirit of the Alberta Indian Treaties*, (University of Alberta Press, Edmonton, 1987), p. 115.

2. David Hall, *"A Serene Atmosphere? Treaty 1 Revisited,"* Canadian Journal of Native Studies, vol. IV, no. 2, 1984, p. 324. (Words in italics at request of author.)

3. John L. Taylor in R. Price, ed., *The Spirit of the Alberta Indian Treaties*, p. 7.

4. Alexander Morris, *The Treaties of Canada with the Indians of Manitoba and the Northwest Territories*, pp. 285-292. (Words of clarification in parenthesis by author.)

5. Hugh Dempsey, *Big Bear The End of Freedom*, (Douglas and McIntyre, Vancouver, 1984), p. 109.

6. John Tobias in Getty, Ian and A. Lussier, *As Long as the Sun Shines and Water Flows*, (University of British Columbia Press, 1983), p. 43. (Words of clarification in parenthesis by author).

7. Stand Cuthand in Ian Getty and Don Smith (eds.), *One Century Later*, (University of British Columbia Press, 1978), p. 34.

8. John Foster in R. Price (ed), *The Spirit of the Alberta Indian Treaties*, p.183.

9. Jean Friesen, *Magnificent Gifts: The Treaties of Canada with the Indians of the Northwest 1869-76, Transactions of the Royal Society of Canada*, series V, vol 1, 1986, p.51.

CHAPTER FOUR

1. Government of Canada, *White Paper on Indian Policy*, (Queens Printer, Ottawa, 1969), p. 11.

2. Ibid, p. 11.

3. *1973 Claims Policy Statement*, pp. 11-12.

4. Ibid, pp. 1-2.

5. Billy Diamond in Menno Boldt and R. Long, *The Quest for Justice, Aboriginal Peoples and Aboriginal Rights*, (University of Toronto Press, 1985), pp. 276-277.

6. Ibid, p. 280.

7. Ibid. pp. 281-82.

8. H. A. Feit in B. Morrison and R. Wilson (eds.), *Native Peoples: The Canadian Experience*, (McClelland and Stewart, Toronto, 1986), p. 203.

9. 1990 Department of Indian and Northern Affairs statement on specific claims.

CHAPTER FIVE

1. Section 35 (1), (2) of Constitution Act, 1982.

2. Fifth Report of the Standing Committee on Aboriginal Affairs and Northern Development on Consideration of the implementation of the "Act to amend the Indian Act" as passed by the House of Commons June 12, 1985, (Queens Printer, Ottawa, 1988).

3. Government of Canada, *Indian Self-government in Canada, Report of the Special Committee*, (Queens Printer, Ottawa, 1983), p. 12.

4. Policy Statement on Comprehensive Land Claims, (1986), p. 8.

5. Pocklington, Tom, *Government and Politics of Alberta Metis Settlements*, (Canadian Plains Research Centre, Regina, 1991).

6. Verna Kirkness, *Indian Control Over a Decade Later*, MOKAKIT, (1984), p. 78.

7. Chief Crowe's comment on Cliff Wright.

CHAPTER SIX

1. British Columbia Court of Appeal, *Saanichton Marina Case*.

2. John Ciaccia, *The Settlement of Native Claims*, (The Alberta Law Review, vol. XV, Edmonton, 1977), pp. 556-562.

3. R. Fisher and W. Ury, *Getting to Yes, Negotiating Agreement Without Giving In*, (Penguin Books, New York, 1983), p. 13. (Words in italics at request of author.)

4. B. S. Slattery, *Understanding Aboriginal Rights*, (The Canadian Bar Review, vol. LXVI, 1987), p. 783.

5. Harold Cardinal, *The Rebirth of Canada's Indians*, (Hurtig Publishers, Edmonton, 1977), p. 149.

6. Government of Canada, *A Report of the Commissioner on Indians*, (Queens Printer, Ottawa, 1977), p. 17.

7. Canadian Bar Association, *Aboriginal Rights in Canada: An Agenda for Action*, (1988), p. 58.

8. *Unfinished Business, An Agenda for All Canadians in the 1990s*, Standing Committee on Aboriginal Affairs, (Queens Printer, 1980), p.30.

9. Supreme Court of Canada, *R.E. Sparrow vs Her Majesty the Queen*, (May, 1990), p. 24.

EPILOGUE

1. Spicer Commission's List of Questions for Citizens Forums, 1991, p.1.

2. Pearl Calahasen, Task Force Member.

3. Alberta's Constitutional Task Force Report, 1991, p. 15-16.

4. Price, 1987, p. 114, translated from Cree to English by Harold Cardinal.

Glossary ─────────────────

Aboriginal Original, indigenous or first peoples of an area. The earliest inhabitants of a country.

Aboriginal rights Special rights held by aboriginal people, such as the right to fish and hunt game.

Abolish To put an end to, terminate or delete.

Activist A person that takes direct action in support of or in opposition to a controversial issue.

Adhesion Agreement or consent to an existing agreement.

Agenda The items of business to be dealt with at a meeting.

Ambiguity The possibility of two or more meanings to the same thing.

Amending formula The procedure that must be followed to make any changes to a constitution.

Amicably In a peaceful or friendly manner.

Annuity A sum of money payable yearly.

Archive A place in which public records or historical documents are kept and preserved.

Assimilate To absorb one group completely into the culture of another.

Autonomous Self-governing.

Band The legal definition given to distinct groups of Indian clans and families by the Indian Act.

British North America Act A statute enacted on March 29, 1867 by the British Parliament providing for the Confederation of Canada.

Cede To give up, yield or surrender.

Chief Factor The head of a fur trading organization in a particular location.

Civil servant A person who works for the government.

Clan Any group of relatives or associates.

Coercion The act of restraining or dominating by force or threat of force.

Commissioners Members of a group authorized to perform certain official duties or functions.

Compensation Payment or reimbursement for goods or services received.

Confederation The union of the colonies of British North America to form Canada.

Confirm To assure the validity of something or to remove doubt by an authoritative act.

Confrontation Challenging or meeting in a hostile manner.

Constitution The core system of rules and principles by which a nation or group is governed.

Consultation The act of asking advice of or seeking council from another.

Controversial Questionable or open to disagreement.

Criteria Standards for making a judgement.

Deficit The amount by which a sum of money made falls short of the amount of money spent.

Delegate To entrust to another.

Deplete To use up or run out of.

Enfranchise To gain full legal status as a citizen of a country or member of a group.

Ethnocentric The attitude that one's own group or culture is the most important.

Expansionists Members of a political organization in Ontario which advocated expansion into western Canada.

Expenditure The amount of money spent from time to time.

Famine An extreme scarcity of food leading to widespread starvation.

First Ministers' Conference A meeting of the prime minister and provincial premiers.

First Nations The Indian people and their descendants.

Fraud An act of deceiving or misrepresenting.

Grievance Cause for complaint.

Guardian One who is put in charge or in trust of a person or persons.

Habitat The place where a plant or animal naturally lives or grows.

Implement To carry out or accomplish.

Incorporate To unite into one body.

Indian Act The principal federal statute dealing with Indian status, local government and the management of reserve lands and communal monies.

Indian assets claims To assert that Indian monies or resources held in trust by the government were not properly managed or improperly disposed of.

Indian Claims Commissioner A senior official appointed to investigate and report on Indian claims.

Indigenous Living or occurring naturally in a region.

Inherent The essential character of something.

Integrate To unite with something else.

Jurisdiction The power, right or authority to interpret and apply the law within a given territory.

Land surrender claims To assert that surrenders of Indian reserve lands were illegal or improper.

Mandate An authorization given to a representative to do something.

Marginal Barely useful or acceptable.

Mandatory An obligation or command.

Marauder One who raids or loots.

Meech Lake Accord The 1988 agreement made by the federal government and the provinces regarding amendments to the Canadian Constitution. The document was signed in Meech Lake, Quebec.

Memorandum of Agreement A written record of some issue or arrangement that concerns two or more governments.

Metis People of mixed North American Indian and European ancestry..

Millennium A period of a thousand years.

Minor A person who is under the age at which he/she is recognized by the law.

Monarch The ruler or head of state.

Moratorium A pause in action on an issue.

Municipal Local, county, town or city government.

Negotiate To consult with another to arrive at the settlement of some matter.

Obligation Something one is required to do.

Oral accounts Historical events and stories passed on by word of mouth.

Patriation To bring under the direct control of the country for which it was intended.

Perpetual Continuing forever.

Post-secondary transfer program Partial programs begun in one institution or school which can be carried on in a post-secondary institution or school.

Reciprocal To return equally or in kind.

Relinquishment To give up or pass over.

Reprisal Retaliation against another.

Reserves in severalty Reserves for small families.

Residential schooling Schools created by churches and the federal government where Indian students had to reside for the duration of their schooling.

Rituals Established ceremonies.

Royal Commission An official inquiry appointed by Parliament to look into matters of public concern.

Scrip A certificate which entitles the holder to land or money.

Sovereign Supreme authority over land or people.

Symbolism The use of something that stands for or represents something else.

Task Force A group of people appointed to investigate or report on a given task.

Theory A probable explanation based on observation and reasoning on the way things work.

Transform To change in character or condition.

Treaty A contract, settlement or agreement arrived at by negotiations.

Treaty land entitlements Indian claims for reserve lands that have not yet been given under the treaties.

Trustee One appointed to manage the affairs of another.

Vested Placed in permanent possession or control of a person or persons.

Select Bibliography ━━━━━━━━━━━━━━━━━━━━

Allen, Robert and Tobin, Mary. *Native Studies in Canada: A Research Guide.* (3rd edition) Indian and Northern Affairs. Queens Printer. Ottawa, 1989.

Asch, Michael. *Home and Native Land.* Methuen Publications. Toronto, 1984.

Assembly of First Nations. *Traditions and Education Towards a Vision of our Future.* 3 Volumes. Education Secretariat, Assembly of First Nations. Ottawa. 1988-89.

Barman, Jean, Hébert, Y and McCaskill, D. *Indian Education in Canada, Volume I The Legacy.* University of British Columbia Press. Vancouver, 1986.

Barman, Jean and Hébert, Y, and McCaskill, D (Eds). *Indian Education in Canada Vol II, The Prospect.* University of British Columbia Press. Vancouver, 1987.

Berger, Thomas. *Northern Frontier, Northern Homeland.* Douglas & McIntyre. Vancouver, 1989.

Berger, Thomas. *Village Journey.* Hill and Wang. New York, 1985.

Boldt, Menno and Long R. *The Quest for Justice, Aboriginal Peoples and Aboriginal Rights.* University of Toronto Press. Toronto, 1985.

Cardinal, Harold. *The Rebirth of Canada's Indians.* Hurtig Publishers. Edmonton, 1977.

Cardinal, Harold. *The Unjust Society.* Hurtig Publishers. Edmonton, 1969.

Carter, Sarah. *Two Acres and a Cow: Peasant Farming for the Indians of the Northwest, 1889-97. Canadian Historical Review.* Vol LXX, Vol II. 1989.

Cassidy, Frank and Bish, R L. *Indian Government, Its Meaning in Practice.* Institute for Research on Public Policy. Victoria, 1989.

Ciaccia, John. *The Settlement of Native Claims.* Edmonton, The Alberta Law Review. Vol XV.

Cox, Bruce. *Native People, Native Lands.* Carleton University Press. Ottawa, 1987.

Cumming, Peter and Mickenberg, Neil. *Native Rights in Canada* (2nd ed). General Publishing. Toronto, 1972.

Dempsey, *Hugh, Big Bear The End of Freedom,* Douglas and McIntyre, Vancouver, 1984.

Dempsey, Hugh. *Crowfoot, Chief of the Blackfoot.* Hurtig Publishing. Edmonton, 1972.

Dempsey, Hugh. "*Isapo-muxika (Crowfoot)*", *Dictionary of Canadian Biography,* Vol. XI. University of Toronto Press. Toronto, 1982.

Dempsey, Hugh. "*Pitikwahanapiwiyin (Poundmaker)*", *Dictionary of Canadian Biography,* Vol. XI. University of Toronto Press. Toronto, 1982.

Elias, Peter Douglas. *The Dakota of the Canadian Northwest.* University of Manitoba. Winnipeg, 1988.

Erasmus, Peter. *Buffalo Days and Nights.* Glenbow Alberta Institute. Calgary, 1976.

Fifth Report of the Standing Committee on Aboriginal Affairs and Northern Development on Consideration of the implementation of the "Act to amend the Indian Act" as passed by the House of Commons June 12, 1985, Queens Printer, Ottawa, 1988.

Fisher, R and Ury, W. *Getting to Yes Negotiating Agreement without Giving In.* Penguin Books. New York, 1983.

Flanagan, Thomas. *Some Factors Bearing on the Origins of the Lubicon Lake Dispute.* Alberta (Journal). Vol. 2., No. 2. 1990.

Foster, J.E. *Indian-White Relations in the Prairie West During the Fur Trade Period — A Compact?* in R. T. Price, editor, *The Spirit of the Alberta Indian Treaties.* Univeristy of Alberta Press, 1987. pp. 181-200.

Frideres, James. *Native Peoples in Canada Contemporary Conflicts.* 3rd edition. Prentice Hall. Toronto, 1988.

Friesen, Jean. "*Magnificent Gifts: The Treaties of Canada with the Indians of the Northwest 1869-76,*"*Transactions of the Royal Society of Canada,* Series V, Vol. I, 1986.

Friesen, Jean. *Morris, Alexander, Dictionary of Canadian Biography,* Vol. XI. University of Toronto Press. Toronto, 1982.

Friesen, Gerald. *The Canadian Prairies, A History.* University of Toronto Press. Toronto, 1984.

Fumoleau, Rene. *As Long as this Land Shall Last.* McClelland and Stewart. Toronto, n.d.

Getty, Ian and Lussier, Antoine. *As Long as the Sun Shines and Water Flows*. University of British Columbia Press. Vancouver, 1983.

Getty, Ian and Smith, Donald. *One Century Later: Western Canadian Reserve Indians Since Treaty 7*. University of British Columbia Press. Vancouver, 1978.

Goodwill, Jean and Shuman, N. *John Tootoosis*. Pemmican Publications. 1984.

Government of Canada. *A Report of the Commissioner on Indian Claims*. Queens Printer. Ottawa, 1977.

Government of Canada. *Indian Self Government in Canada, Report of the Special Committee*. Queens Printer. Ottawa, 1983.

Government of Canada. *Indian Treaties. The Archivist.*, November-December, 1989. Vol 16. No. 6. Queens Printer. Ottawa.

Government of Canada. *Living Treaties: Lasting Agreements* (Report of the Task Force to Review Comprehensive Claims Policy). Queens Printer. Ottawa, 1985.

Government of Canada. *Treaties One, Two, Three, Four, Five, Six, Seven, Eight, Nine, Ten* and *Eleven*. Queens Printer. Ottawa.

Government of Canada. *White Paper on Indian Policy*. Queens Printer. Ottawa, 1969.

Grant, J. W. *Moon of Wintertime Missionaries and Indians of Canada in Encounter since 1534*. University of Toronto Press. Toronto, 1984.

Hall, David. "*A Serene Atmosphere? Treaty 1 Revisited*," *The Canadian Journal of Native Studies*. Vol IV, No. 2, 1984.

Hawkes, David (Ed). *Aboriginal Peoples and Government Responsibility, Exploring Federal and Provincial Roles*. Carleton University Press. Ottawa, 1989.

Hawthorn, H. B. *A Survey of the Contemporary Indians of Canada*. 2 Volumes. Queens Printer. Ottawa, 1966-67.

Johansen, Bruce. *Forgotten Founders*. Gambit Publishing. Ipswich, MA,1982.

Johnston, Basil H. *Indian School Days*. Key Porter Books. Toronto, 1988.

Indian Chiefs of Alberta. *Citizens Plus* (Red Paper). Indian Association of Alberta. Edmonton, 1970.

Indian Tribes of Manitoba. *Wahbung, Our Tomorrows*. Manitoba Indian Brotherhood. Winnipeg, 1971.

Laird, David. "*Our Indian Treaties,*" *The Historical and Scientific Society of Manitoba*. Winnipeg, 1905.

Leslie, John and Maguire, Ron. *The Historical Development of the Indian Act*, (2nd ed). Treaties and Historical Research Centre. Indian and Northern Affairs Canada. Ottawa, 1978.

Littlebear, Leroy, Boldt, M and Long, J.A. (Eds). *Pathways to Self Determination, Canadian Indians and the Canadian State*. University of Toronto Press. Toronto, 1984.

Long, J. Anthony and Boldt, M. (Eds). *Governments in Conflict? Provinces and Indian Nations in Canada*. University of Toronto Press. Toronto, 1988.

Madill, Dennis. *Treaty Research Report: Treaty Eight. Treaties and Historical Research Centre*. Indian and Northern Affairs. Canada, 1986.

Mair, Charles. *Through the McKenzie Basin A Narrative of the Athabasca and Peace River Expedition of 1899*. W. Briggs. Toronto, 1908.

Mandelbaum, David. *The Plains Cree, An Ethnographic, Historical and Comparative Study*. Canadian Plains Research Centre, University of Regina. Regina, 1985.

Manuel, George and Posluns, M. *The Fourth World, An Indian Reality*. Collier MacMillan. Don Mills, 1974.

Maslove, Allan. *Canada's North: A Profile*. Statistics Canada. Queens Printer. Ottawa, 1990.

Miller, J R. *Skyscrapers Hide the Heavens, A History of Indian White Relations in Canada*. University of Toronto Press. Toronto, 1989.

Milloy, John. *The Plains Cree, Trade, Diplomacy and War 1790 to 1870*. University of Manitoba Press. Winnipeg, 1988.

Morris, Alexander. *The Treaties of Canada with the Indians*. Coles Publishing Co. Toronto, 1971. (Reprint from original Bedford and Clarke Co. of Toronto, 1880.)

Morrison, Bruce and Wilson, R. *Native Peoples: The Canadian Experience*. McClelland & Stewart. Toronto, 1986.

Morse, Brad (Ed). *Aboriginal Peoples and the Law: Indian, Metis and Inuit Rights in Canada*. Carleton University Press. Ottawa, 1990.

Nin, Da. Waab, Jig. (Jacobs, Dean). *Minishenhying Anishnaabe-aki, Walpole Island: The Soul of Indian Territory*. Walpole Island Indian Band. Wallaceburg, Ontario, 1987.

150

Owram, Doug. *Promise of Eden, The Canadian Expansionist Movement and the Idea of the West 1856-1900*. University of Toronto Press. Toronto, 1980.

Peterson, Jacqueline and Brown, J. *The New Peoples: Being and Becoming Metis in North America*. University of Manitoba Press. Winnipeg, 1985.

Pocklington, Tom. *Government and Politics of Alberta Metis Settlements*. Canadian Plains Research Centre. Regina, 1991.

Ponting, Rick (Ed). *Arduous Journey, Canadian Indians and Decolonization*. McClelland and Stewart. Toronto, 1986.

Price, Richard. *Claims Negotiations and Settlement: Fort Chipewyan Cree, Alberta and Canada* in *Proceedings of the Fort Chipewyan and Fort Vermilion Bicentennial Conference*. Editors McCormack, P., and Ironside, G. Boreal Institute for Northern Studies. Edmonton, 1990.

Price, Richard (Ed). *The Spirit of the Alberta Indian Treaties*. University of Alberta Press. Edmonton, 1987.

Ray, Arthur. *Indians in the Fur Trade, Their role as hunters, trappers and middlemen in the lands southwest of the Hudson Bay 1660 - 1870*. University of Toronto Press. Toronto, 1974.

Salisbury, Richard F. *A Homeland for the Cree, Regional Development in the James Bay*. McGill-Queens University Press. Montreal, 1986.

Slattery, BS. *Understanding Aboriginal Rights*. The Canadian Bar Review. Vol; LXVI, pp. 727-783.

Saskatchewan Indian Cultural College. *Treaty Six* . Saskatoon, 1980.

Stanley, George. *The Birth of Western Canada*. University of Toronto Press. Toronto, 1962.

Standing Committee on Aboriginal Affairs. *Unfinished Business: An Agenda for All Canadians in the 1990s*. Queen's Printer. Ottawa, 1990.

Surtees, Robert. "*Canadian Indian Treaties*," *History of Indian-White Relations*. Smithsonian Institution. Washington, 1988.

The Great Law of Peace of the People of the Longhouse. White Roots of Peace. Akwesasne, New York, 1972.

Taylor, J.L. *Canada's Northwest Policy in the 1870s: Traditional Premises and Necessary Innovations*, in R. T. Price, editor, *The Spirit of the Alberta Indian Treaties*. University of Alberta Press. Edmonton, 1987. pp. 3-7.

Taylor, K Lynn. *Thinking Development in the Context of a Mainstream Subject Area*. Unpublished MA thesis. Dalhousie University. Halifax, 1989.

Titley, Brian E. *A Narrow Vision, Duncan Campbell Scott and the Administration of Indian Affairs in Canada*. University of British Columbia Press. Vancouver, 1986.

Tobias, John. *Protection, Civilization, Assimilation: An Outline History of Canada's Indian Policy*, in Getty, I.A.L and A.S. Lassier, *As Long as the Sun Shines and Water Flows*. University of British Columbia Press. 1983. pp. 39-55.

Tobias, John. "*Canada's Subjugation of the Plains Cree, 1879-1885*." *Canadian Historical Review*. Vol. LXIV. 1983.

Vanstone, James. *Athabascan Adaptations: Hunters and Fishermen of the Subarctic Forests*. Aldine Publishing Co. Chicago, 1974.

Weaver, Sally. *The Making of Canadian Indian Policy*. University of Toronto Press. Toronto, 1981.

Wilmsen, Edwin N. *We Are Here, Politics of Aboriginal Land Tenure*. University of California Press. Berkeley, 1989.

Wolfe, Alexander. *Earth Elder Stories*. Fifth House Publishers. Saskatoon, 1988.

Zaslow, Morris. *The Opening of the Canadian North 1870 - 1914*. McClelland and Stewart. Toronto, 1971.

Index ─────────────────────────────

A

Aboriginal rights, 100, 102-103, 109
Aboriginal rights claims, 78, 82, 93, 113
Agriculture, 34, 51;
    Treaty Six negotiations, 50;
    written treaty promises (chart), 55, 57
Ahanakew, Edward, 72
Alliance of First Nations, 116
Annuities, 51
    written treaty promises (chart), 55, 57
Assembly of First Nations, 108-109, 111
Athabasca Landing, 34, 35
Athabascans, 28, 30

B

Barber, Lloyd, 130
Berger, Thomas, 130
Big Bear, 59-60
Bill C-31, 104
Blackfoot, 12, 20, 65;
    territory of (map), 29
Bourassa, Robert, 87
British Columbia Court of Appeal, 124
British North America Act (1867), 8, 69, 79
Buffalo, 19, 59-60
Burrows, Acton:
    on Indian wars, 15-16

C

Cadieux, Pierre, 120
Canadian Bar Association, 130
Cardinal, Harold, 79, 83, 128
    Address to Queen (1973), 84
Charter of Rights and Freedoms, 103, 105
Chief Factor, 11
Chipewyan, 28-29, 31, 42
    territory of (map), 29
Citizens Plus, (*See* Red Paper)

Claims Policy Statement (1973), 83, 88, 94
Clark, Joe, 101
Comprehensive claims, 93
Constitution, 100-101, 103, 111
Constitution Act of 1982, 103;
    key sections, 102
Cote, J. Arthur, 38
Council of Yukon Indians, 90
Courtorielle, Lawrence, 96
Cree, 40-41, 60;
    Fort Chipewyan, 95-97;
    James Bay, 87-90;
    Plains, 19-20, 22;
        territory of (map), 29;
    Woodland, 22, 28-29, 40;
        territory of (map) 29
Cree Naskapi of Quebec Act (1984), 112
Chrétien, Jean, 79, 82, 116
Crowfoot, 12-13, 73

D

Dakota, 6
Dawson, S. J.:
    on oral history, 50
Day schools, 66
Dene, 28, 40
Dene-Metis of the Northwest Territories, 90-91
Diamond, Billy, 88-89

E

Education, 43, 51, 65, 75-76, 108;
    band-operated schools, 116 (graph), 119;
    day schools, 66;
    government and churches' view of, 66;
    Indian control of, 116-117;
    industrial schools, 66;
    Post Secondary Student Assistance Program, 120;
    post-secondary, 76, 119-121;

residential schools, 66, 75;
    written treaty promises (chart), 54, 56
Expansionists, 15-16

F

Faulkner, Hugh, 119
Federation of Saskatchewan Indians, 72
First Ministers' Conferences, 101, 103, 114, 124;
    on Treaty and Aboriginal Rights and the
    Constitution (1987), 108
Fishing:
    written treaty promises, 54, 56
Fort Carlton, 11, 22
Fort Chipewyan, 29, 39, 42, 95, 97
Fort Chipewyan Cree, 95, 96, 97
Foster, John:
    on significance of fur trade, 11;
    on Indian sense of betrayal, 72
Frank, Alex, 70
Friesen, Jean:
    on treaty fulfillment, 73
Fur trade, 10, 11, 28-31;
    Hudson's Bay Company, 29, 31, 32;
    Northwest Company, 29;
    trading posts (map), 30

G

Grandin, Vital, 32
Great Law of Peace of the People
    of the Longhouse, 4, 5

H

H'damani, 6
Harper, Elijah, 104, 105
Harvard University's Negotiating Project, 128
Health care, 42, 43, 50, 108;
    at trading posts, 31;
    written treaty promises (chart), 54, 56
Hind expedition, 16, 17
Hudson's Bay Company, 29, 31, 32;
    trading posts (map), 30
Hunting:
    written treaty promises, 54, 56

Hydro-electric development:
    James Bay, 87, 88;
    James Bay II, 90

I

Indian Act, 61-62, 67, 72-73, 75, 103-104,
107-108, 112-113, 117;
    of 1876, 64;
    legislation:
        Indian resistance to, 67
Indian Affairs (Department), 34, 65, 94, 107,
    114, 121
Indian Agent, 64-65, 67
Indian asset claims, 94
Indian Association of Alberta, 72, 83;
    Red Paper, 79
Indian First Nations, 76, 109, 111-112, 114,
    124, 126
Inuvialuit, 90

J

James Bay and Northern Quebec Agreement
    (1975), 89, 90, 93
James Bay Cree, 87-90
James Bay II, 90

K

Kihewin, 19, 20
Kinosayoo, 32;
    at Treaty Eight negotiations, 40-41
Klondike Gold Rush, 35-36

L

Lacombe, Albert, 40-41
Laird, David, 13, 15, 38-42, 61, 64
Land surrender claims, 94
Land scrip, 38
Land:
    claims, 93;
    written treaty promises (chart), 55, 57
League of Indians of Canada, 72
Lesser Slave Lake, 32, 34-35, 39, 40

Little Pine, 60
Loft, Fred, 72
Lorne, Marquis of, 59, 73

M

Macdonald, John A., 16
MacKenzie River Valley Pipeline Inquiry, 130
Manuel, George, 79
McKenna, D.A.J., 38, 42
McKnight, William, 120
Meech Lake Accord, 104-105
Metis, 10-11, 30, 38-39, 60, 102-103, 107
Missionaries, 31-32, 38, 40
Mistawasis, 25
Money scrip, 38-39
Moostoos, 40-41
Morris, Alexander, 12, 15, 22, 25, 50

N

National Indian Brotherhood, 116
Natural Resources Transfer Agreements, 61, 69;
    excerpt, 69
Nelson, J. C., 62
Nishga Indians of British Columbia, 82, 91
North West Mounted Police, 12-13, 35-36, 38
Northwest Company, 29;
    trading posts (map), 30

O

Office of a Treaty Commissioner, 121
Ojibwa, 6, 24-25;
    territory of (map), 29
Oral accounts, 1-2, 20, 22, 49-50

P

Palliser expedition, 16, 17
Palliser triangle (map), 17
Parliamentary Standing Committee on
    Aboriginal Affairs, 120-121, 131
Penner Report, 108, 111-112,
Penner, Keith, 111
Piapot, 60
Plains Cree, 19, 20, 22;
    territory of (map), 29

Pontiac, 6-7
Post-Secondary Student Assistance Program,
    120
Poundmaker, 24, 25
Prairie Treaty Nations Alliance, 108-109
Prospectors, 35-36

Q

Quebec Boundaries Extension Act (1912),
    87-88
Queen Elizabeth, 83, 101, 103;
    Reply to Indian Association of Alberta
    (1973), 85
Queen Victoria, 51, 84, 85

R

Railway, 16, 28
Red Paper, 79;
    Summary comparison to White Paper (chart),
    80-81
Report of the Special Committee on Indian Self-
    Government in Canada (See Penner Report)
Residential schools, 66, 75
Reserves in severalty, 39-40
Reserves, 22, 24-25, 38, 43, 51, 61-62, 95;
    in severalty, 39-40
Ross, J. H., 38;
    Treaty Eight negotiations, 41, 42
Royal Commission, 130-131
Royal Proclamation of 1763, 6, 7, 8, 82,
    103, 109

S

Saddle Lake, 62, 72
Scott, D. C., 69
Scrip Commission, 38-39
Scrip Commissioners, 38
Scrip, 38-39
Sechelt band, 112, 114, 116
Sechelt Act, 113
Seenum, James, 62
Self-determination (See self-government)
Self-government, 76, 103, 104, 105, 107, 108,
    109, 111, 112, 113, 114, 116-117
Settlement, 19, 28, 50;
    expansionist movement, 15

Seven Years' War, 6
Sifton, Clifford, 40
Smallpox, 19, 20, 31
Specific claims, 93-94
Stanley, George, 21-22;
    on written history, 2
Star Blanket, 25
Supreme Court of Canada, 8, 70, 82-83,
    124, 125,
Sweetgrass, 19, 20

T

Time for Action, A, 100
Tobias, John:
    on Indian Acts, 61-62
Trapping, 61, 28, 70;
    written treaty promises (chart), 54, 56
Treaty adhesions, 42
Treaty areas (map), 52-53
Treaty commissioners, 8, 23, 41, 50, 62;
    Laird, 13, 15, 38, 39, 40, 41, 42, 64;
    McKenna, 38, 42;
    Morris, 12, 15, 25, 50;
    Ross, 38, 41, 42
Treaty Eight, 28, 38-43, 95;
    area (map), 44-45;
    events leading up to, 34-36;
    written treaty promises (chart), 56-57
Treaty Eleven:
    written treaty promises (chart), 56-57
Treaty Five:
    written treaty promises (chart), 54-55
Treaty Four:
    written treaty promises, 54-55
Treaty land entitlements, 69, 70
Treaty land entitlement claims, 93, 94, 95-97
Treaty making:
    among European nations, 6;
    between Indian peoples, 4, 6
Treaty Nine, 43;
    written treaty promises (chart), 56-57
Treaty negotiations, 7-8;
    Elders' accounts of, 22-24;

Federal government's goals, 48;
    in northern Canada, 38-42;
    Indian peoples' goals, 48
Treaty of Paris (1763), 6
Treaty on Migratory Birds (1916), 61
Treaty One, 24;
    written treaty promises (chart), 54-55
Treaty Seven, 12-13, 23-24;
    written treaty promises (chart), 56-57
Treaty Six, 11-12, 22-23, 25, 50;
    excerpt of, 20;
    written treaty promises (chart), 56-57
Treaty Ten:
    written treaty promises (chart), 56-57
Treaty Three, 24;
    written treaty promises, 54-55
Treaty Two, 24;
    written treaty promises, 54-55
Trudeau, Pierre Elliott, 78, 79, 83, 100, 101
Tuberculosis, 66
Tungavik Federation of Nunavut, 90

U

United Nations, 124

W

Wahbung, Our Tomorrows, 79
Walker, James, 38
Western development, 15-16, 17
White Paper on Indian Policy, 78, 79, 83;
    summary comparison to Red Paper (chart),
        80-81
Wolfe, Alexander:
    significance of oral tradition, 1-2
Women's rights, 103, 104
Wood Buffalo National Park, 95
Woodland Cree, 22, 28-29, 40
    territory of (map), 29
Wright, Cliff, 121
Written history, 2, 20
Written treaty promises (chart), 54-57

About the Author

Richard T. Price is an Associate Professor at the School of Native Studies, University of Alberta. He served as the first Director of the school from 1986 to 1991.

Professor Price holds Bachelor degrees in Commerce and Theology and a Masters of Arts degree in Political Science. In addition, he has worked for almost twenty years with Alberta Indian peoples, and done research in the areas of Indian treaties and land claims.

Indian and Inuit Communities
in Canada